S†RANGERS

PETER HECK

Library of Congress Cataloging-in-Publication Data

ISBN-13: 978-1532942174
ISBN-10: 1532942176

Published in the United States by
Attaboy Press

a division of Attaboy Productions, Inc.
2139 Emily Court
Kokomo, IN 46902

For more information on Attaboy Productions, Inc., please visit:
www.peterheck.com

Distributed in cooperation with
CreateSpace
7290 B. Investment Drive
Charleston, SC 29418

This book is dedicated to my Grandpa Jean, a heroic veteran of both earthly and eternal battles

CONTENTS

STRANGERS

In a Strange Land

1
NOTHING NEW

It had been a pretty good day when I sat down in front of my laptop to check my email. Big mistake. I began scrolling through the handful of "you suck, please die" responses to a recent newspaper column, as well as the always entertaining pleas from random foreign hackers that beg:

> "Help me, I'm stranded in Madagascar after being robbed at gunpoint by a posse of rabid African badgers and need you to drain your savings to help me get to the American embassy."

First of all, if I have a friend so dumb that they chose to vacation in Madagascar, it's probably best they just stay stranded. What they apparently need more than my financial help is some time isolated on an island to think through their poor decisions that led them there in the first place. Besides, how do I know that the armed badgers aren't standing there waiting to take all my money that I wire them? And why are they emailing me? Why didn't they just send the email directly to the American embassy to come and help them? And surely they know me better than to think I have any money to send anyone. No, I think Scripture is clear that if your friends are that dense, best to delete the email and help them learn to make better life choices. I think that's what Jesus would do.

Anyway, I continued perusing my inbox and came upon a message that would take that good mood of mine and smash it into a thousand depressed little pieces.

I've redacted the name of this Christian brother and will hereafter refer to him only as Brother Eeyore. He wrote:

> "We are forsaken and judged. We are hopeless and lost. In every corner of our society there is a menagerie of rebellious spirits who pull the mindless masses towards the pit of eternal Hell. We are a people of unclean lips and deserve every bit of the judgment that is now unfolding upon us. We have chosen rebellion, we have chosen evil, we have chosen vice, and God has turned His back on every one of us. I cannot blame Him. I cannot press our case. We have no case. We have no justification. We are to be hurled down to the pit of despair that awaits all nations that disobey the word of the Lord. An appeal to mercy or grace is but a slap in the face of the Almighty. We had our chance and chose to worship worthless idols – all of us – and now we reap what we have sown. We are disowned and abandoned to our own folly and will soon taste the bitter fruits of our deceit as our bodies are singed by the initial flames of unyielding torment. This is how our great American experiment ends."

STRANGERS

After reading that I felt I had no choice but to head straight out to the garage, wrap my lips around the exhaust pipe of the minivan and punch that remote starter button.

Don't get me wrong, I certainly agree with Eeyore about the sorry state of the culture we live in. We are truly living out the very pages of the Apostle Paul's book of Romans. Seriously, let me quote just a few lines from the first chapter of that book and you tell me if it isn't a picture-perfect description of modern America.

> For although they knew God, they neither glorified him as God nor gave thanks to him, but their thinking became futile and their foolish hearts were darkened.

If images of frat parties and college raves attended by formerly churched youth raised in homes that were adorned with Scripture references on walls and required church attendance every Sunday don't enter your mind, you aren't thinking. These young people know God, they just don't fear Him or revere Him. They show no gratitude for His provision and no concern over His providence, and therefore indulge all kinds of evil.

> Although they claimed to be wise, they became fools.

Does this not describe our people? One of the most astounding statements I have ever seen on national television occurred when *CBS News* was doing a segment on how a Boulder, Colorado police officer accidentally shot and killed the town's beloved elk. The townspeople held a candlelight vigil for the deceased deer singing songs like, "We Shall Overcome" and "Amazing Grace."

Just before the segment ended, an unidentified (thankfully, for her sake) woman was interviewed. And in a flawless depiction of the very kind of moral foolishness that masks itself as wisdom these days, this lady protested, "And I don't see a whole lot of difference between the shooting of this defenseless elk and the shooting of schoolchildren in Connecticut."

Despicable? Yes. Clueless? Yes. To even begin to utter a statement equating the death of a big deer with the merciless slaughter of innocent and precious Kindergarteners at Sandy Hook Elementary School requires such a level of moral stupidity that the only word that can be applied to it is "fool."

Therefore God gave them over in the sinful desires of their hearts to sexual impurity.

If Martians were watching American society from a long-range telescope, there is not much doubt that they would conclude the words "Sexual Impurity" were a far more accurate national motto to adorn our currency than "In God We Trust."

After all, we live in a society where mayors of major cities[1] as well as leading officials on large university campuses[2] tell *Chick-fil-A* that they can't operate in their respective jurisdictions because the chicken shop "doesn't share our values." These cities and universities are objecting to this statement made by *Chick-fil-A*'s CEO, Dan Cathy:

> "I think we are inviting God's judgment on our nation when we shake our fist at Him and say, 'We know better than you as to what constitutes a marriage.' I pray God's mercy on our generation that has such a prideful, arrogant attitude."[3]

Those words received scorn from the same culture where men like pornographic *Playboy* founder Hugh Hefner, who infamously bragged to Time Magazine that, "It is easier to deal with several girlfriends than one wife,"[4] is honored with the "Founder's Hero of the Heart Award"[5] and whose documentary wins an "Image Award"[6] from the NAACP.

Sexual immorality is so lauded these days that the same society where political science professors like Marquette's John McAdams face termination for defending the right of free speech on the topic of homosexuality,[7] while institutions like Indiana University build massive research facilities honoring depraved child molesters like Alfred Kinsey (the man who ran sexual experiments on toddlers to try to provoke them to orgasm).

For the degrading of their bodies with one another.

When I hosted a weekly radio show on the largest talk radio station in Indiana (WIBC), I tried to get the outgoing Republican Mayor of the city, Greg Ballard, to consent to an interview. I wanted to ask him why he felt it was appropriate for him to act as the Grand Marshal of the Indianapolis [Gay] Pride Parade.

I had never been to the Indy Pride event before but had seen plenty of pictures. I'd also read the eyewitness testimony of those who had attended it and other so-called "Pride" events. The best I could figure, these were largely abhorrent displays of hedonism and sexual anarchy. Patrick Craine wrote of his experience at the Ottawa Pride Parade,

> "While the majority of parade *watchers* are dressed rather normally, among those walking in the parade it was not odd at all to see semi-nudity and hyper-sexualized dancing. There were loads of people in nothing but underwear, dozens in leather bondage gear, and I saw at least a dozen topless women. I took everything I was handed, and walked away with a dozen condoms. Having now attended, I would describe Pride as a *large-scale, state backed celebration of kinky sex.*"[8]

7

1 NOTHING NEW

And it's about that latter part that I wanted to question Mayor Ballard. Even if the Mayor lacks the moral or political backbone to forbid voyeurism and decadence on the streets of his city, why is it necessary or even appropriate to give tacit approval and embrace of it?

The Mayor didn't come on my program to answer that question. But he did serve as Grand Marshal of the parade, issuing statements about how the event somehow reinforced the image of "Hoosier Hospitality." Yes, because nothing warmly welcomes visiting families to downtown like subjecting them to city-sanctioned close encounters with grown men in dog collars and leather G-strings dry humping the air.

Few in our culture and certainly not our elected leaders are willing to say it, so I will. These parades are gross. They're not okay. And, to be frank, they in no way represent all people with same-sex attraction anymore than a parade of pornographers would represent all with opposite-sex attraction. Not long ago, lesbian feminist activist Julie Bindel expressed this very frustration of many in the homosexual movement. "[Pride parades] became about sexual hedonism," she scolded, insisting that the only message sent by these modern spectacles of self-indulgence is, "this is just one great party all about sexual access to as many other men as we can secure."[9]

And our culture's media, from national news broadcasts to cable to local TV stations, all celebrate it. In Indianapolis, I was amazed at how local broadcasts selectively displayed pleasant images of young children with rainbow face paint along the parade route. There was no mention of the parade attendees wearing t-shirts that read, "tight butthole," no footage showing barely-covered men sexually thrusting themselves against poles on their float in full view of children, no expression of concern at the gender-bending drag queens in fishnets who in years past have walked throughout the crowd handing out condoms and lube to anyone regardless of age.

STRANGERS

Forget love. The entire point of these parades is to provide sorry adults an opportunity to regress into infantile immaturity and immorality. It's an excuse to lose themselves in their own lusts and celebrate their carnal desires. And we applaud this as behavior to take "pride" in?

Maybe this is what happens when your civilization begins taking its cues on appropriate human behavior from the intellectual insights of circus acts like Lady Gaga. When your people begin calibrating their moral compass by juvenile song lyrics of women that dress up in meat suits for award shows, perhaps it should come as no surprise when elected mayors join the dominatrix and bondage brigade.

But whatever the cause, there is one thing that is unquestioned: the degrading of our bodies is not just an occurrence these days. It's celebrated with "pride."

They exchanged the truth about God for a lie.

Famed physicist Lawrence M. Krauss recently stood before a group of fellow atheists and dismissively mocked the Creator of the natural world he studies. A woman in the audience asked him whether his field of physics was a "safer haven" for atheists than other realms of science like biology. The implications of her question can't be overlooked. Implicit in her inquiry is the revelation that atheist scientists desire to be insulated from any notion of the supernatural. That which they cannot explain or understand, they feel compelled to dismiss. Don't overlook the startling arrogance of such a position. And I would contend it's an arrogance that most of them don't apply consistently.

When arguing with atheists about the existence of God, I often pose questions to them that they simply can't answer. It's one thing to say all the matter of the universe was confined to a tiny pinpoint of dense light and then it exploded or expanded rapidly at the moment of the Big Bang (or singularity). But the question remains, where did the matter in that pinpoint of light come from? Every atheist I've ever asked this question to responds the same way: "I don't know."

I'm guessing Krauss and this female questioner would say the same. They would recognize that with as bright as they may be, their intellect falls woefully short of understanding the breadth and depth of all the mysteries of our universe. In fact, they say that's what makes science fascinating. While I would agree, the 600 pound gorilla is sitting there staring them in the face unnoticed: "Isn't it possible that in the vast amount of mystery to the universe that you don't know, that a supernatural God could exist to bring meaning and purpose to much of what you have studied and discovered?"

Which brings us back to the stunning and revealing response that Krauss gave this woman:

> "Most scientists don't think enough about God to even know if they're atheists. God is just irrelevant. So it's not as if physics or biology are one or more safe than the other. God doesn't enter into it ever."[10]

Prominent intellectuals and leading scientists like Krauss then are not making a reasoned rejection of the truth of God based on evidence, they are engaging an *a priori* (before the fact) rejection of His existence before their study begins. Conclusions they draw, then, can only affirm that which was originally assumed.

What does that mean? It means that if God does exist, they have willfully exchanged His truth...for a lie.

> *They have become filled with every kind of wickedness, evil, greed and depravity. They are full of envy, murder, strife, deceit and malice.*

Want proof? Turn on the 11 o'clock news tonight.

STRANGERS

They are gossips, slanderers, God-haters, insolent, arrogant and boastful.

I remember sitting in my jeep one Michigan morning in the summer of 2015. I was waiting to head in to speak at a church camp and was listening to a radio program that happened to be covering the presidential campaign announcement of Donald J. Trump. I was laughing as the cohosts of the program kept interjecting with humorous comments about this joke candidacy. After all, this is a tycoon who actually says things like:

> "It's hard for them to attack me because I'm so good looking."[11]

> "I could stand in the middle of 5th Avenue and shoot somebody and I wouldn't lose voters."[12]

> "Why do I have to repent or ask for forgiveness, if I am not making mistakes? I work hard, I'm an honorable person."[13]

> "I'm not sure I have ever asked God's forgiveness. I don't bring God into that picture."[14]

Surely a civilization that rejects the arrogant and boastful would have no part of such a campaign, right?

They invent ways of doing evil.

ESPN – the macho sports network – just recently gave out their "Courage Award," to a man wearing lipstick, high heels and an evening gown. He still spoke with his masculine voice, and he still had his male genetic identity. But an entire network, and seemingly an entire sports community, has decided to find honor in boys pretending to be girls.

Consequently, city councils are passing laws and

11

ordinances opening up bathrooms and locker rooms where little girls are showering and dressing to grown men to do the same. Seriously, could you have ever predicted something so crazy would be happening here? We truly are inventing ways of doing evil that no one had ever thought of before.

Look back at those italicized statements I just listed. Forget for a moment that they come out of the ancient book of Romans and you could easily be convinced that they were lifted from some social conservative, Christian website lamenting the current state of our country.

So while I understand and sympathize with Brother Eeyore's frustration, I fear he and all of us who are tempted to think like that are missing something critical: God isn't surprised by what is happening around us. He knows very well where the wickedness of man's heart can lead a people estranged from His truth. It is, after all, the story of humanity. And each time that sorry narrative begins to unfold onto the pages of our history, God intentionally interrupts man's march to oblivion by sending His chosen servants to stand against the rising tide of immorality.

Maybe the reason you picked up this book is because you are one of the chosen.

2
ENEMY OCCUPIED
TERRITORY

The truth? What's happening in America these days has been a long time coming.

Even Depression-era author John Steinbeck pinpointed our impending decline with remarkable candor when he wrote, "Now we face the danger which in the past has been most destructive to the human: success – plenty, comfort, and ever-increasing leisure. No dynamic people has ever survived these dangers."[15] He concluded that ours was a country on the, "verge of moral and hence nervous collapse."[16]

It's not a difficult concept when applied to other areas of life. A basketball team humiliated by an embarrassing season works and drills continuously in the offseason to improve. The next year they begin experiencing tremendous success, and the program is solid for years to come as those veterans of the team (who had been witness to the effort required to achieve greatness) continue pushing to sustain it. But after those players move on, the expectation of success becomes an enemy to those who don't know the sacrifice it requires. The values of hard work and effort are forgotten, and consequently time in the gym is replaced with time in front of the camera. The collapse is imminent and predictable.

The principle is as old as...well, the Old Testament, where Moses cautioned the Israelites,

> "When you have eaten and are satisfied, praise the Lord your God for the good land he has given you. Be careful that you do not forget the Lord your God, failing to observe his commands, his laws and his decrees that I am giving you this day. Otherwise, when you eat and are satisfied, when you build fine houses and settle down, and when your herds and flocks grow large and your silver and gold increase and all you have is multiplied, then your heart will become proud and you will forget the Lord your God, who brought you out of Egypt, out of the land of slavery. He led you through the vast and dreadful wilderness, that thirsty and waterless land, with its venomous snakes and scorpions. He brought you water out of hard rock. He gave you manna to eat in the wilderness, something your ancestors had never known, to humble and test you so that in the end it might go well with you. You may say to yourself, "My power and the strength of my hands have produced this wealth for me." But remember the Lord your God, for it is he who gives you the ability to produce wealth, and so confirms his covenant, which he swore to your ancestors, as it is today.
>
> If you ever forget the Lord your God and follow other gods and worship and bow down to them, I testify

against you today that you will surely be destroyed. Like the nations the Lord destroyed before you, so you will be destroyed for not obeying the Lord your God."[17]

If the principle was true for the Israelites, if it was true for that basketball team, it stands to reason Steinbeck was right to properly observe it would be true for us as a civilization. That's why in recent years we've seen the warning signs: (1) the number of Bible-believing Christians diminish, (2) the rise of secular statists and their legal bulldogs demanding the isolation of religious principle from the public square, and (3) the increasing number of magazine headlines that scream, "The Decline and Fall of Christian America"[18] or "Why Are Christians Losing America?"[19]

But despite the warnings, many believers have been caught off guard by our cultural rebellion against God, and are therefore experiencing a wide range of emotional reactions to it – from anger to frustration to panic to dismay. I'm pretty sure Brother Eeyore experienced all of those in just one paragraph. But while these emotions are natural and excusable human responses to being thrust into unexpected and uncomfortable surroundings, I worry it can also reflect a deeper misunderstanding or confusion about our citizenship as Christians.

What I mean can best be explained by the second observation we must make relative to this cultural decline we are experiencing in America. And that is: it's nothing new for God's people.

It may be new for American believers given our unique history in a country founded largely on a Judeo-Christian ethic, but from Rome to Corinth to Canaan, the encompassing story of God's followers on earth is one that mirrors exactly what we're encountering today.

As but one example, consider the response of the famous

Corinthian escort (prostitute for the wealthy) Lais when a Christian confronted her about her behavior. According to the historian Athenaeus, Lais responded, "What is foul if it seems not so to those who indulge it?"[20] In other words, what makes something bad or wrong if those who are doing it like it? Or, "Who are you to tell me what we're doing is bad if we like to do it?"

Sound a wee bit familiar? It should. After all, if Lais was still around, she could sue Grammy winner Sheryl Crow for plagiarism. It's Crow who now croons the words to one of her hits, "If it makes you happy, it can't be that bad." See what I mean? What we are experiencing is nothing new.

In many ways, we American Christians are just now beginning to find ourselves where God's people have always been – not in the lap of cultural comfort, but in the heat of cultural conflict. Nearly every page of Scripture is filled with the exploits of one of God's chosen confronting the godlessness around them. Whether it's Noah preaching to his wicked generation, Moses stalking Pharaoh with God's demands, Elijah mocking the false prophets of Baal, Jonah agitating the status quo in Nineveh, John the Baptist crying out for truth in the wilderness, or Esther daringly opposing the King's highest officials who planned to exterminate her people, the storyline is powerfully similar.

So similar that it leads the observant among us, like the great thinker C.S. Lewis to conclude,

> "Enemy-occupied territory – that is what this world is. Christianity is the story of how the rightful king has landed, you might say landed in disguise, and is calling us to take part in a great campaign of sabotage."[21]

Simply put, we shouldn't be surprised that things are falling apart around us. And when we accept that it obviously is, our response shouldn't be, "Oh no! What do we do?!" It should be, "Well of course it is, it's the world after all." This is our story and we should embrace it not with depression but rather motivation.

The great Apostle Peter wrote these words in his first book:

> "To God's elect, exiles scattered throughout the provinces of Pontus, Galatia, Cappadocia, Asia and Bithynia, who have been chosen according to the foreknowledge of God the Father, through the sanctifying work of the Spirit, to be obedient to Jesus Christ and sprinkled with his blood: Grace and peace be yours in abundance."[22]

You may be utterly clueless about the identity or relevance of those cities he mentions, but take note of the term he uses to describe God's chosen: "exiles." This letter of Peter is directed to Christ-followers who had been scattered, providentially by God, as exiles throughout a hostile world.

I don't believe those are words meant for believers at that time only. I think they are meant for us. We are now the exiles. We are now the scattered few. And we are being called to obedience, not under the pressures of isolation and frustration, but with the assurance of God's grace and peace.

Saying all that is tough to squeeze into one email response. So rather than try, I sent back this simple reply to Brother Eeyore instead:

> "Friend, if you are called by the name of Christ, this place isn't your home. I don't quote Jesus now as a rebuke, but as an encouragement:
>
> 'Do not let your hearts be troubled. You believe in God; believe also in me. My Father's house has many rooms; if that were not so,

would I have told you that I am going there to prepare a place for you? And if I go and prepare a place for you, I will come back and take you to be with me that you also may be where I am.'[23]

You believe in God. You believe in Jesus. Let your thoughts reflect that."

Two days later I got this back from him: "I guess I need to get used to being a stranger in a strange land, huh?"

Yep.

STRANGERS

3
WE ARE STRANGERS

It's a little odd that the notion of being "strangers" is such a foreign concept to Christians these days. I say it's odd because that is the key principle behind surrendering your life to Christ. Peter writes,

> "Praise be to the God and Father of our Lord Jesus Christ! In his great mercy he has given us new birth into a living hope through the resurrection of Jesus Christ from the dead, and into an inheritance that can never perish, spoil, or fade. This inheritance is kept in heaven for you, who through faith are shielded by God's power until the coming of the salvation that is ready to be revealed in the last time."[24]

When you surrender to the Lordship of Christ, it is also a surrender of citizenship in this world. We no longer belong to the world, no longer place our hope in the world, no longer find our inheritance in the world. Everything we have or lay claim to is held for us in heaven – our new homeland. We quite literally become citizens of heaven. The moment that happens, and the more we grow in our faith, this world (regardless of our cultural surroundings) begins to feel foreign and unsettling.

When I first began teaching, my room was right across the hall from the French class at our school. One day, for reasons I'm not quite sure, I found myself perusing the various France travel guidebooks the teacher had on her shelves. One of them caught my eye for being remarkably useless. While it did offer basic English to French translation for key words, it also had a separate section boasting "important phrases" that a visitor to France might need quick access to. I can't remember them all, but there were a few that were so ridiculous that they became a running joke between me and my colleague. Phrases like:

"What smell is that?"
"I can't move my leg."
"Give me a high five."

I can't imagine a situation arising on my French vacation where I would ever need to know any of those phrases. Isn't there a universally understood face-scrunch you make when you want to know what stinks? If I'm trapped beneath some massive collapsed steel beam with a crushed femur, isn't it likely that the French paramedics are probably going to be able to deduce that I've got a leg issue? And do the people of France still do "high fives?" If so, maybe I don't want to go after all.

There was also a section in the book for male-to-female pick-up lines. Ladies, imagine being a French woman minding your own business when some clown comes walking up to you with a guidebook in hand and says in broken dialect, "Can I have your picture so I can show Santa what I want for Christmas?" Is that dude not asking for a merciless public beating? Wait, maybe that's why the "I can't move my leg" phrase was included.

StRANGERS

Anyway, if you've ever been to a foreign country (with or without a guidebook), you know the feeling of isolation. Even in other English speaking countries it is palpable. You look different, you sound different, you aren't at ease, you stand out.

And truthfully, you don't have to leave the country to experience that feeling. About a year ago I found myself walking the streets of Indianapolis the same week that some comic book convention was in town. I walked into Chipotle for lunch and thought I had stepped into the bar scene from Star Wars. It was a weird feeling being in normal street clothes yet feeling like *I* was the weird one.

Older folks have told me that's the kind of feeling they get living in a world of iPhones and androids. I'll never forget going with my grandparents to supper one evening. They had a brand new car and were very proud to show it off. But with as much as they liked it, both of them lamented how technological everything had become. Grandpa talked about how he just doesn't understand technology and doesn't like it. Before long I was hearing from both of them how they were content to just have a car that gets them from point A to point B in relative comfort – they don't need flashy. About that time the windshield wipers popped up and swiped the perfectly dry windshield. Given that there wasn't a cloud in the sky or rain in the forecast, I asked Grandpa what just happened. Nonchalantly, this man who just got done telling me how uncomfortable he was with technology proceeded to tell me that he had set the wipers to sense moisture accumulating on the windshield and automatically trigger rather than being forced to do it manually. You know...just like in the old days.

But with as much as I gave him a hard time about that, I do sympathize with those who grew up in the era of chalkboard slates as they attempt to adjust to the high tech world of sim cards. One of the biggest complaints I hear from grandparents and even parents about their kids is the new "text-language" as they call it, with abbreviated terms and acronymic phrases:

LOL – laugh out loud
BRB – be right back
NP – no problem
NUB – a new person

They complain they can't keep up or understand this "foreign language." I've actually encouraged these older folks rather than be annoyed and attempt to fight the new language, they should embrace it in a way that turns the annoyance around on their children and grandchildren. Start coming up with their own cryptic phrases like others have to send to one another:

BFF – best friend fell
GGPBL – gotta go pacemaker battery low
FWIW – forgot where I was
ROFLACGU – rolling on the floor laughing and can't get up

Making their punk kids feel as out of place as they do seems like a laudable goal to me. Unfortunately that hasn't seemed to catch on at this point.

But these feelings of awkward isolation, whether from technology, comic book conventions or traveling out of the country, are precisely the feeling Christians should experience in this world.

Normally I keep busy enough that I have to have someone else approve comments that people make to my various articles on my website. But one day over Christmas break, I was handling it myself and came across a remark submitted by a former student of mine named Brandon. He chastised,

"I have to say you have really gone over the edge with the conservative thing. The sooner America embraces a secular existance (sic) and crawls out of the dark age we are mired in where religious superstition supercedes (sic) common sense, the sooner real progress can begin. I for one will not be a slave to a God that does not exist, or more accurately, I will not bow to the various cults that attempt to use this myth of God to force their agenda on others."

It's always good to hear from former students, although the powers of observation do not appear very strong in this one. I responded:

"Hey Brandon, great to hear from you. Truth is America has embraced and is embracing a "secular existence." Not sure how you could look around our society and believe otherwise. Also not sure how you can look at the most advanced civilization in world history and conclude we are mired in the "dark age."

But I also understand you have an irrational hatred towards Christianity and so it's easier to lob rhetorical bombs than apply the same level of skepticism to your own worldview as you apply to mine. So be it. I do hope you are well and have a Merry Christmas...or whatever non-cultish celebration you may be engaging in this season. All the best."

Polite, I thought...with a hint of deserved sarcasm. But what I wrote was certainly true – this is a secular culture in every way. No doubt Brandon and others would point to the statistics from Pew or other research companies that show roughly 70% of Americans call themselves Christian.[25] When someone tells me that, I compare it to my experiences on social mediums like Facebook and Twitter that have taught me there is a very high percentage of the population that view themselves experts on politics, sports and entertainment. Yet, their asinine observations and critiques would certainly indicate otherwise.

Similarly there are people who call themselves Christian who haven't cracked open a Bible in decades, haven't gone to church since the Reagan years and believe it's totally irrelevant whether God created the world in 6 days or the Big Bang did it in, what's it up to now…11, 12, 13.7 billion years (forgive me that by the time this book goes to print, the highly respected "scientific community" will probably have decided they need a few more billions in there to obfuscate some other piece of evidence that contradicts their story).

The real number of Bible believing Christians in the United States is way, way less than it is portrayed. Before she left the mindless gabfest on ABC called "The View," veteran reporter Barbara Walters quoted from the highly respected Barna Group:

> "Only 1% of the youngest adults, 18-23, has a
> 'Biblical worldview' which is that the Bible is
> completely accurate and Satan's a real
> being…only 1% of young adults and only 9% of
> all American adults has a Biblical worldview,
> that is that the Bible is completely accurate."[26]

First, these numbers make far more sense. If 70% of the population were truly Bible believing Christians, our culture wouldn't look as it does. Pornography wouldn't be seen as harmless free speech, divorce wouldn't be such an acceptable pastime, cheating wouldn't be regarded as being clever and resourceful, greed wouldn't be honored as ambition, and child killing wouldn't be championed as women's rights.

But secondly, these numbers should drive home a very important point to true believers. If you are young and Christian, 99% of your peers don't think like you. If you're an adult and Christian, 91% of your peers don't think like you. Once you realize that, things that have been frustrating you start to make sense.

It's what keeps me sane and smiling when people post comments on my newspaper articles like, "Heck is the same as a Nazi," "Mr. Heck and his hate are probably headed for Mr. Hell" (yes, someone actually wrote that), and "Heck is nothing more than an idiot, and an unintelligent one at that" (who knew there was such a thing as an intelligent idiot?).[27]

But on a more serious note, this reality also provides clarity as to why you may feel like so many Christians want to throw you under the bus when all you're doing is standing for the authority of Scripture. It's not you doing anything wrong. It's that they don't really believe in the authority of the Bible.

I remember being online shortly after the Supreme Court issued their infamous gay marriage dictate and being sickened by the number of alleged Christ followers who had adopted the rainbow overlay for their Facebook avatar. Why would people who supposedly know the physical and spiritual consequence of living an unrepentant homosexual lifestyle find it wise, prudent or loving to affirm and encourage such behavior in those they supposedly care about?

Probably for the same reason that the faculty council at Wheaton College, formerly one of the country's leading Christian institutions, unanimously defended the tenure of Professor Larycia Hawkins when she was exposed for teaching the unquestionably heretical and anti-Biblical belief that Christians and Muslims worship the same God.[28]

Probably for the same reason that Serene Jones, the president of Union Theological Seminary, a Christian university where famed theologians like Dietrich Bonheoffer have lectured, could come on my radio program and defend the practice of child killing:

SJ: Ten years ago we developed a socially

responsible investing policy that divested us from tobacco, and from firearms and from alcohol.

I think if you were to look at the leading, one of the leading causes of death in the country today of young people, um, you would be in one of those three categories.

Um, and we're also in the process of looking into our investments – if we have any, we're exploring this right now – in for-profit prisons, that are in a sense making money off of imprisonment.

So we take very seriously a whole range of issues. And, as a board, and as a whole community, we discussed them extensively.

PH: Mmm-hmm. I would say that when you're talking about young people, obviously, abortion would seem to be one of the leading causes of killers of children. And I think as a Christian university that would be another great position for UTS to take.

To say, you know, we're not going to invest in companies that are funding, that are supporting the destruction of God's innocent – we talk about creation meaning the earth, but God's most innocent creations in the womb, in the sanctuary of the mother's womb, certainly that seems like a great place for UTS to take a stand as well.

Any chance that that might happen?

SJ: Well, you know, when I think about, particularly women and fertility, um, we have just begun to scratch the surface in terms of our scientific work around the impact of climate change on fertility.

And particularly in poor countries where you're living in a toxic environment where you have bodies that never even have the possibility of imagining having the choice to reproduce. And I think that's very serious and it's just going to continue to increase until we as a globe take on what our toxic environment is doing to the bodies of everyone, and in particular the reproductive bodies of women. It's a, it's a, it's a massively important point for us to put into this conversation.

PH: Uh yeah, I definitely want the bodies of women to be cared for as well as men to be cared for. And that isn't just the grown ones. And it isn't just the toddlers. It isn't just the infants. But it's that innocent life in the womb as well.

And I just, I feel like maybe um, you're not wanting to answer my question relative to the unborn. And I guess that's where I sit back and just say "Aren't we warped when we're going to take such a firm stand on protecting an environment but we're not going to take a similar stand of importance when it comes to protecting innocent human life.

SJ: I, you and I are just going to disagree on that, um –

PH: But I guess, why? That's maybe my biggest question. Why not…

SJ: Sure, I mean you wanna have a theological discussion about it? I don't want to talk about it politically but I can sure talk about theologically.

PH: You mean about life in the womb?

SJ: Yes! So tell me your, your theological reasons based on God and Scripture um for this position and I'll respond to you theologically.

PH: Okay, absolutely, let –

SJ: Let's do it, let's do it in the context of Calvin, come on, let's go!

PH: Okay, well here –

SJ: I'm ready!

PH: First and foremost, I guess maybe I need to ask you, what do you believe is conceived in the womb? Is it a human being?

SJ: (pregnant pause) Is conceived in the womb?

PH: Yes.

SJ: Um (pregnant pause), I think that you would have to say that what is conceived in the womb, if you go to Scripture and you look at the history of Christian tradition on this point, the amount of change that has um, been associated with that – so at the time of Jesus when Scripture was written, you were not considered to be pregnant until you had had what was called 'quickening.'

And quickening was the first time that the mother could feel the child move in the womb.

And that was for about 800 years the standard that the church used to determine you know, what the point of conception was. That was the point that people believe God breathed the spirit into the life and it sprung into being.

PH: Okay, and that's what you believe?

SJ: Um, you know, I that that; I think that what we see is that the idea of when conception occurs has changed.

In my mind, um, uh, then we're talking about the point of quickening, I think the point at which we begin to think about it consciously, um, I think that before quickening when we talk about what happens in the womb of a woman, everything is in such process at that point too.

So, we can continue to talk about this.

PH: Uh, I, I guess –

SJ: So what would you say, what would you say about the view that in Jesus' time there was no indication whatsoever that there was some magical point of conception before quickening? I mean, how do we address that in –

PH: Well, first of all –

SJ: Relation between Biblical times and our times today?

PH: Right. You can go back before the time of Jesus. You can go back into the Old Testament law, the law of Moses where if a man attacked and was physically assaulting a woman and caused her to have premature birth – the baby

was born prematurely – then he would be
fined, so on and so forth.

If there was further damage then the 'eye for an
eye,' 'tooth for tooth,' 'life for life' law applied.
So even before the days of Jesus in the Old
Testament law code you have the notion of the
unborn baby being a human being that
constituted a man losing his life if the life of
that child is lost.

And certainly throughout Scripture you see
repeatedly that the life conceived in the womb
is constantly referred to as a baby, not, not
anything else.

And I guess even from a scientific standpoint
today, we can talk about quickening, we can talk
about all of that, but from a scientific
standpoint today, attempting to mark the start
of human life anywhere but the point of
conception becomes a fool's game.

It becomes drawing an arbitrary line in the sand
where we try to say, "Okay well at this moment
it's a human being but before that, well, what
was it? A fern?"

And if we say it's going to be the moment of
birth, well is that when the first body part
comes out of the womb? Is it when the baby
draws the first breath and then the second
before that it's not a human being?

It gets into this silly calculation that I think is
much more indicative of someone trying to
justify an immoral act than it is actually
pursuing truth and consciously understanding

the issue.

Which is, I guess where I wanted to go with all of this. If we're taking a stand on moral ground as Christians, and we're standing for – which what I think you're trying to do wIth this act at UTS – I just don't grasp why a university taking such a firm stance in our culture would be ashamed to take that stand when it comes to God's innocent creations.

SJ: And I think we're just going to disagree on this.

PH: Very good.

SJ: We live in a very tragic world.

PH: There's no question about that, no question. Serene I appreciate your time very much.

SJ: Okay, thank you.[29]

How can Christians possibly disagree on whether child killing is morally permissible? How is that even debatable amongst Jesus followers? These are the kinds of things that can make you go crazy until you recognize the truth I just mentioned: 91% of my fellow American adults don't believe in Biblical authority. And that truth manifests itself in a profound feeling of isolation, a feeling that we don't belong with those that surround us, often even in the church pew.

So how do we respond? Recognizing the extent to which we are foreign and seemingly alone can tempt us towards negativity, depression and silence. But read the very next verse in that passage from 1 Peter I quoted at the start of this chapter:

"In all this you greatly rejoice, though now for a little while you may have had to suffer grief in all kinds of trials."[30]

How is that even possible for us to greatly rejoice in such circumstance? I'm glad you asked.

4
NOT ABOUT POLITICS

In the United States, politics has become god.

That point really isn't debatable when you consider the ungodly amounts of money that are spent on campaigns for public office. According to the FEC, 7 billion dollars were spent on the 2012 presidential campaign between Mitt Romney and Barack Obama – more dollars than there were people on the planet.[31] That's insane.

Of course when you realize that those campaigns now start nearly two full years before the actual ballots are cast, it starts to add up. But remember, that's only presidential campaigns. Factor in every state and local election across the country, like the 2002 race for Bergen County Executive in New Jersey that saw nearly $18 million spent,[32] and your eyes will start to cross.

And even non-elected positions have become consumed

with politics. Every time a Supreme Court justice dies or retires from the bench, it becomes wall-to-wall coverage on our politically-obsessed 24-hour cable channels.

This is a fairly simple phenomenon to explain, actually. Politics is the pursuit of power. Regardless of how it is used or delegated, politics is the art of chasing power and influence. And when man replaces God with himself, when there is no transcendent moral authority to which all men are accountable, power becomes the ultimate objective.

Take a playground with no adult supervision or authority. A power struggle always commences and results in the rise of a bully. Every child on the playground then has a vested interest in observing that bully and whether he will be their protector or their foe.

That perfectly explains the obsession Americans have over their political environment. And Christians aren't to be caught up in any of it.

Now, I say this not to be critical of Christians who observe, comment on, or engage in politics. Anyone who knows me knows that I am a political junkie – a guy who rocked a 4.0 all the way through grad school to earn a Masters of Arts in political science. I find the field fascinating, I find it important, and I find it more entertaining than the vast majority of people I know.

When I say Christians shouldn't be "caught up in it," what I mean is that we shouldn't "absolutize" politics. It is not of highest value or importance, and those who find success in the political world are not demigods or philosopher-kings.

To the contrary, they are flawed and fallen individuals in whom we should place no more hope than we do our next-door neighbor. If you're getting your favorite politician's face tattooed on your chest, fainting at the sound of their voice, or

chucking your child's college tuition money at their campaigns, that's a pretty good sign you've got an emotional attachment that is bordering on unhealthy.

And it's this kind of emotive investment in the realm of politics that can be very dangerous for Christians. We can easily find ourselves forgetting our citizenship in heaven and replacing our true King with an earthly one. We stop looking strangely and bizarrely at those pagans among us who deify earthly leaders, ordaining them with ornamental robes and gold-crusted crowns, and begin imitating them with our own "chosen one."

We soon find ourselves less concerned with the Word of God and more concerned with pop culture sloganeering that calls us to be "on the right side of history."

What an utterly moronic concept. What is history, after all? C.S. Lewis said it best:

> "All that we call human history – money,
> poverty, ambition, war, prostitution, classes,
> empires, slavery – is the long, terrible story of
> man trying to find something other than God
> which will make him happy." [33]

Given such a proper definition of human history, it's fair to say that there is no "right side" to it in the first place. No, being on the "right side of history" isn't anything Christians concern themselves with because we recognize history isn't God. God is God. History isn't our Judge. God alone is Judge. And therefore, our behavior must conform to His standards, not history's; His expectations, not historians'; His will, not those who would deign to be history makers'.

This then is the focal point of the Christian life. Loving a God who loved us first despite all our shortcomings, we joyfully (there are no unhappy saints) seek to influence this world towards Him. This action is motivated by our love of God, not a love of power.

When this becomes your proper focus, do you know what you quickly realize? Any attempt to influence others crosses freely into the realm of politics. Properly understood, politics, like every other area of the Christian life (education, literature, entertainment, music, science) is an avenue to transmit Truth. And just like in each of those other areas, Christians are to use the field of politics to glorify God, not self.

Meaning, regardless of whether it's popular or mainstream, regardless of whether it profits us, we will always oppose any effort or cause that denies the Natural Law and Moral Order of the Real King, that denies the dignity and worth of life made in His image, or that denies the individual or corporate freedom of man to worship his Creator.

Is it likely that opposing such things will lead us as Christians into political conflict? Of course! Look at modern American culture for proof:

When the enduring truth of marriage is being stripped of its meaning in the name of sexual anarchy, the Moral Order of God is certainly being undermined.

When medical professionals are delivering healthy children before snipping their little spinal cords with scissors and discarding these babies with medical waste, the dignity and worth of life made in God's image is being trampled.

When churches and individual believers are facing fines and punishment from the government over their allegiance to Biblical standards of sexual morality, the individual and corporate freedom of man to worship is being challenged.

As Christians, we are to boldly and confidently engage those conflicts, flavoring the debate with the salt of truth. We must always remember our purpose in such conflict is not vanity or personal aggrandizement, but rather to bring glory to

God.

Sadly, God's people are too often bullied into silence (even by their own), being told things like, "The church's responsibility is to lead sinners to Christ, not to engage issues of rights and public policy." Biblically, those two responsibilities are not mutually exclusive. You needn't give up your testimony to Christ's salvation to defend defenseless babies. And you needn't give up your stand for religious liberty to lead someone to Jesus.

If Jesus was right when He told the Roman Governor Pilate that all earthly authority comes only by the will of God,[34] then surely it is ludicrous to suggest that God's truth should not be heard in matters of earthy authority. But if it should be heard, precisely who will voice it if His followers do not?

Remember the account of Paul addressing the court of Festus in Acts 25, where he challenges the authorities:

> "If the charges brought against me by these
> Jews are not true, no one has the right to hand
> me over to them. I appeal to Caesar!"[35]

What is happening here? Those opposed to the spread of the gospel of Christ were attempting to silence Paul's testimony to the truth of God's word. And notice Paul didn't retreat into the cultural shadows. He didn't slink back home and say, "I think God is trying to tell me to influence people through simple acts of kindness, generosity and friendship...just by 'showing the love of Jesus.'" No, Paul didn't acquiesce and withdraw his public testimony to the privacy of the local church.

He knew the law, used the law, and demanded to plead for his rights in the highest courts of Caesar. But notice why he did – notice his purpose. It was not to consolidate power for himself or his friends. It was to further expand the proclamation of the message of Jesus. That is Christian political engagement as God intends. Engaged for the purpose of glorifying Him and spreading His truth to the world.

S†RANGERS

5
LOVING THE NASTY
COMMENTS

Struggling to resist a nefarious, godless, evolving rebellion against God that is unfolding around us certainly isn't fun at times. You'd have to be insane to actually enjoy being called a bigot, a hater, or many of the other loathsome titles being hurled towards Bible-believers these days.

But it's important to remember that our Christian brothers and sisters in the first century not only had to endure scorn and mockery for their faith, but also got the added bonus of being beaten, imprisoned and decapitated as well. And yet remember it was the Apostle Peter himself, shortly before being crucified for speaking truth, who wrote these words:

> "In all this you greatly rejoice, though now for a little while you may have had to suffer grief in

all kinds of trials."[36]

But how? And why? Why should God's people rejoice in the times of conflict we endure? Though there are undoubtedly more, I can think of two primary reasons.

First, the grief we encounter clarifies to everyone the character of God's enemies on earth. Shortly after the U.S. Supreme Court ruled in the now infamous case of *Obergefell v. Hodges* that same-sex couples could legally "wed" in all 50 states regardless of the will of the people, I received a massive amount of taunting emails that each demonstrate precisely what I am talking about.

One sneered,

"You are a *expletive expletive*, and you and all your *expletive* loser *expletive* Christian friends can *expletive* off. It's over, *expletive*. You lost, love won, and you can *expletive* die and burn in hell for all I care. #LoveWins"

Having received emails from this potty mouth previously, I am confident this was not a parody account or a joke correspondence. No, this was the hilarious self-contradiction that comes when you willfully suppress the truth in all unrighteousness.[37]

It apparently didn't even dawn on the activist who wrote the email that it is the height of absurdity to characterize your movement and message by the moniker of "love" when you managed to squeeze seven profane expletives into three short sentences. The soul of anyone who could author such a literary masterpiece could be defined with many adjectives, but "loving" is probably not one of them.

A second email read,

"Finally! Science has triumphed over your

backwards religious book of fairy tales. Finally we can live in the 20th Century."

I thought we backwards religious types were the ones supposedly living in the past? It's the 21st Century and this guy has evidently just made it into the 20th. But beyond that, the appeal to science in defense of the so-called gay rights movement is intellectually vapid.

After all, it is science, that has been decidedly unable to find any evidence or data that indicates a biological or chemical origin for homosexual conduct. It is science that has confirmed through repeated inquiry and evaluation that homosexual tendencies are not innate or immutable characteristics, but rather a psychological manifestation affected by nature and environment. Thus, it is mindless to attempt to scientifically equate sexual preference with biological origin.

But it's worse than that. This anti-truth, anti-God sexual rebellion is a movement that would tell you in one breath that sexual attraction and preference is something that is innate, inborn and unchangeable. If you are attracted to girls that can never be tamed or turned. If you are attracted to boys, that's "who you are" and can't be changed. In fact, this movement is so convinced of some fixed reality of sexual preference that they now seek government-imposed bans on counseling, that includes psychiatric assistance for those who want to combat their same-sex attraction.

In 2015, the city council in Cincinnati passed an ordinance that levied a $200 a day, $6,000 a month fine against any Christian counselor who offered psychiatric help to a young person struggling with same-sex attraction.³⁸ The very movement that demands everyone's sexual wishes and desires be respected exhibits no respect for the sexual wishes and desires of those who don't want their same-sex impulses. These purveyors of fake tolerance are so disrespectful of the sexual preference of those resisting same-sex attraction that they actually make it illegal for them to seek help.

Further, while activists like the author of this email pretend to be on the side of science, how scientific is it to believe that something as fluid as sexual attraction is unchanging, while something as unchanging as gender is fluid? It's patently absurd for those who claim that a person's sexual attraction *can't* be changed to simultaneously suggest that a person's gender *can* change simply by putting on a dress and mutating their genitals.

Science indeed.

Still another email taunted,

"Step one, check. Equal rights for all. Now, if I can just be honest, I can't wait til we are able to lock all you *expletive* hater Christians up for speaking your hate."

See what I mean by "clarifies the character of God's enemies?" Time and again those who posture in our society as champions of tolerance, acceptance and love, demonstrate they are the most intolerant, unaccepting and hateful people towards those they disagree with politically, religiously or culturally. After all, how can you claim to be an advocate of "equal rights for all" when you are simultaneously calling for Christians to be denied their equal rights and thrown into jail?

But as annoying and frustrating as it may be to suffer grief from those kinds of emails, they are remarkably useful in painting in bright neon colors the intellectual and moral bankruptcy of those who oppose God. Calmly, rationally, even humorously illustrating that to a watching world is exceedingly useful and effective for our cause.

Secondly, the grief we endure as believers helps purify and refine Christ's church, separating the wheat from the chaff and sheep from goats. When biblical belief becomes the subject of ridicule, and even an offense worthy of legal punishment, it unquestionably provokes a great falling away from the faith.

Those whose commitment to Christ has been a casual convenience or mere social service are always quick to compromise, adjust or modify their "beliefs" to fit with prevailing societal winds. They certainly have no intention of suffering for any doctrinal views since they were never truly invested in the intellectual tenets of the faith to begin with. But their betrayal doesn't end there. When fellow Christians refuse to follow the path of capitulation, and instead stand firm on the authority of God's Word over the wisdom of man, the compromisers will be stung with guilt.

To assuage that guilt, they will lash out – not at the oppressors, but at their fellow Christians. To make themselves feel better about their own betrayal, they double down on the name-calling, shaming and demeaning of the faithful being perpetrated by the oppressors. These Christian goats are desperate to be considered sophisticated, rational, and even cool in the eyes of the world. And nothing is more likely to achieve that end than beating up the Christian sheep.

Take the recent example of Kim Davis, the Rowan County (KY) Clerk who despite the Supreme Court's decree on same-sex "marriage," refused to bow her knee to Caesar and participate in the mockery of God by issuing such marriage licenses. The story is well known by now: Davis went to jail for her convictions, served her sentence for defying the court order, was released, and a compromise was reached (thanks to the Davis-supporting Governor Matt Bevin who was elected amidst the furor) that allowed her to keep her name off all future licenses.

But the part of the story often overlooked is how divided the Christian community of the United States was over Davis' incarceration. Those who hold to Biblical authority stood in solidarity with Davis, aghast that our society had reached such a depraved state that it would tolerate the jailing of a gentle, Christian woman simply for honoring God. But casual believers inside the church who reject Biblical authority for the sake of cultural relevance were swift and unforgiving in their indictment of Davis' sins.

Professing Christian blogger and columnist Rachel Held Evans took to Twitter to heap scorn on Davis, writing:

> "No one's being jailed for practicing her religion. Someone's being jailed for using the government to force others to practice her religion."[39]

This is intellectual garbage. Of course Davis was jailed for "practicing her religion," though that is a confusing way of stating it. Davis was put in a position by the state to choose between honoring man's law or honoring God's law. Her faith (allegedly the same one Evans practices) teaches her that when such conflict occurs, she must always choose the latter. So, utilizing the conscience rights afforded to her by the First Amendment, Davis refused to issue the man-ordained licenses. It is bizarre and difficult to conceive how someone as bright as Ms. Evans can misunderstand that fairly obvious reality.

But the second part of Evans' tweet is even more ridiculous. Davis wasn't jailed for using the government to force a gay couple to "practice her religion." That doesn't make any sense. What would that even look like? Davis somehow orders the local National Guard division to force the two gay men into a church pew, stuff communion wafers down their throats and dunk them in the baptistery all at gunpoint? Even at that, a professing Christian like Evans should know that Christianity is not (and can never be) a religion of compulsion. Even in the fanciful scenario I just concocted, those two gay men wouldn't be truly "practicing Christianity." If Evans is ignorant of that, she is ignorant of the core fundamentals of Christianity.

And even a more generous interpretation of Evans' words renders this a stunningly incoherent accusation. There were 129 other locations in the state of Kentucky where the couple practicing homosexuality could have received a marriage license.[40] In other words, even if she wanted to, there was nothing Kim Davis could do to enforce her religious views on anyone. In truth, the aggressors in this account were the couple demanding Davis be forced by the state to violate her conscience. Davis resisted, and fair-weather faith friends like Evans smeared her for it.

And this battle is playing out across the United States. Even in my hometown, our city council recently imposed an anti-First Amendment ordinance that unconstitutionally infringes on the rights of conscience, speech and association for individuals and business owners. It was particularly aggressive towards people of faith, prompting nearly 100 ministers from our community to rally their congregations in opposition.

Yet rising against these Christians' courageous stand for truth and the constitutional right of individuals and businesses to honor God outside the walls of their church building was a group of professing believers (including at least one prominent minister) bastardizing the word of God in order to appear culturally hip. It was an embarrassing spectacle and a spiritual travesty.

Christ's church simply cannot be a potent force for cultural and societal change when it is being led and populated by those who are teaching compromise with the culture and submission to society.

And *that* is why times of grief and struggle can be so beneficial – because it identifies the ear-itching ministers misleading their congregations that otherwise would be very difficult to distinguish.

Here's what the Holy Spirit was conveying to us through

5 LOVING THE NASTY COMMENTS

Peter's pen: in the refining fire of legal, cultural, and sometimes even punitive persecution, those content to live and die by the name of Christ are set apart from those interested in merely wearing it. Having the blessed opportunity to prove which side we're on...that is why we should rejoice.

6
WE ARE THE REAL REBELS

I was having a good conversation with a friend not long ago about the comparisons that could be made between the ungodly rebellions of Old Testament Israel and that of modern America. My friend made many parallels: both had been incredibly blessed by the hand of Providence, both knew better, both were led at times by insufferable egotists, both suffered punishment for their choices.

While those were all fair and accurate points, there remains a major distinction between God's chosen people in Scripture and us today; and it's a difference that should send a chill down our collective spine. We choose our leaders, Old Testament Israel did not.

For all the beauties and benefits of democratic government, it provides a startling reflection of who we are as a people. If we lament an abusive, corrupt and greedy government dominated by self-aggrandizing politicians eager to consolidate power and line their own pockets, what does it say about the people that select those leaders? Who is worse in that equation – the corrupt politicians, or the people who willfully choose them?

In democratic societies, immoral leadership is a clear indication of the immoral character of the masses. If there's any question that is the unpleasant face of popular American culture, consider:

- One out of every four married men in the United States confesses to having at least one extramarital affair.

- More than 70% of men in the United States between the ages of 18 and 34 visit at least one pornographic website in a typical month.

- Approximately one-third of the population of the United States (110 million people) currently suffer from a sexually transmitted disease.

- More than half of all couples in the United States cohabitate before marriage.

- The United States leads the rest of the world in its divorce rate.

- More than half of all children born in the United States to women under 30 are born outside of a married relationship between the parents.

- Approximately one-third of all children born in the United States live in a home without a father.

- The United States has experienced more than 56 million abortions committed since 1973.

STRANGERS

- The United States has the highest incarceration rate in the world.

- The United States has the largest total prison population in the world.

- There are over 60 million Americans that abuse alcohol and 22 million Americans who use illegal drugs.

- There are more than 3 million reports of child abuse a year in the United States.[41] [42]

If that is the face of America (and sadly it is), then it is fairly obvious to even a casual observer that ours is a civilization in complete upheaval against God's moral order. Given that our past includes ancestors and progenitors who proclaimed the importance of maintaining public morality and godly character, that may seem incredible. After all, Charles Carroll of Carrollton, signer of the Declaration of Independence, once wrote to his friend James McHenry,

> "Without morals a republic cannot subsist any length of time; they therefore who are decrying the Christian religion, whose morality is so sublime and pure, [and] which denounces against the wicked eternal misery, and [which] insured to the good eternal happiness, are undermining the solid foundation of morals, the best security for the duration of free governments."[43]

To say recent generations have scorned and dismissed Carroll's wisdom is a bit of an understatement. But that reality shouldn't be a surprise to Christians. This is a pattern that dates back to Old Testament days. In Judges, Samuel writes of Israel:

> "After that whole generation had been

49

gathered to their ancestors, another generation
grew up who knew neither the LORD nor what
he had done for Israel."[44]

Our Founding generations have given way to our own, who
quite apparently know neither the Lord nor what He has done
for the United States of America. The $64 million question, of
course, is why that is the case; what has caused this complete
abandonment of Truth and such disrespect for the Moral
Authority of the Universe? There certainly is no shortage of
experts willing to weigh in on the subject, and yet they each
seem to have come to a different conclusion.

A simple Google search of the question provides
thousands of returns suggesting that our increasing rejection of
God is the result of scientific advancements, Hollywood, the rise
of the internet, pornography, lack of Sunday School attendance,
the public school system, immigration, greed, guns,
multiculturalism, and countless others. Yet despite the eclectic
array of proposed culprits, there is a common theme I notice
running through all of them: they all largely absolve us of any
responsibility in our unfolding collapse. It's "other people's"
fault.

But just maybe there is a simpler answer, albeit an
uncomfortable one. And maybe it isn't difficult to see when we
look through the eyes of Scripture rather than those of a
modern sociologist. Maybe the reason our generation and
those coming after us have forgotten God in our culture is
because we could. Our prosperity led to a complacent faith –
faith never cost us anything, so it hasn't meant anything. And
because it hasn't meant anything to us, it doesn't mean
anything to our teens and young adults.

To say that children model the behavior and beliefs of their
parents is obvious to the point of absurdity. We all chuckle
uncomfortably the first time a child repeats something they
heard us say that we wish they hadn't. And we all smile when

we see a young son with his Little Tikes tool belt following his dad out to the garage to do some work. Even popular songs in both the Christian and secular world highlight this eternal truth. From the Phillips, Craig and Dean hit "Just Like You":

> Lord, I want to be just like You, cause he wants
> to be just like me.
> I want to be a holy example, for his innocent
> eyes to see.
> Help me be a living Bible, Lord, that my little
> boy can read.
> I want to be just like You, cause he wants to be
> like me.[45]

Or the country hit by Rodney Atkins "Watching You":

> A green traffic light turned straight to red,
> I hit my brakes and mumbled under my breath.
> His fries went a-flying and his orange drink
> covered his lap.
> Well, then my four-year-old
> said a four letter word
> That started with "s" and I was concerned.
> So I said, "Son, now where'd you learn to talk
> like that?"
>
> He said, "I've been watching you, dad.
> Ain't that cool?
> I'm your buckaroo, I wanna be like you.
> And eat all my food and grow as tall as you are.
> We got cowboy boots and camo pants.
> Yeah, we're just alike. Hey, ain't we, dad?
> I wanna do everything you do.
> So I've been watching you.[46]

Nothing has a more profound impact on the future ideas and beliefs of a child than the example (or lack thereof) they witness in their parents. Which means if the world is *our* sovereign, we shouldn't be surprised when it is to our children as well.

In his 2014 Erasmus Lecture, the Archbishop of Philadelphia, Charles J. Chaput said it bluntly: "The real problem in America today isn't that we believers are foreigners. It's that our children and grandchildren aren't."[47]

As much of a gut punch as that may be, it's critical that we understand and accept it. Our children become intoxicated by the world because we haven't done our work to show them the distinction between the lies it tells and the truth of God. As a consequence of this occurring for the last few generations, we have become so utterly confused as a society that we regard conformity as rebellion; we treat following the crowd as individuality. Look at college campuses these days. The mass of young people that go there speak in one voice, have one thought, fully embracing the spirit of the age. And yet you will not find a group of people more convinced of their individuality, uniqueness and distinctive originality. It's embarrassing.

I teach in a rural, conservative community, and it half disheartens and half amuses me to watch kids leave our area, go to college and think they have become "rebels" when they eschew and renounce the values of their upbringing. So enamored they become with the siren song of licentiousness that their weak minds are seduced into somehow believing that a collegiate atmosphere far more rigidly dogmatic and doctrinaire than the one they left (it is far easier to be an atheist in rural Indiana than a Bible-believing Christian on campus) offers their overly sheltered souls liberty.

So strong is the indoctrination cult on campus that it doesn't even dawn on their immature intellects that regurgitating the views of their professors and peers, embracing the hedonistic self-worship of pop culture, championing the values of the entertainment industry is not rebellion. It's not authenticity. It's conformity.

STRANGERS

Even the much-celebrated "radical" Saul Alinsky (President Obama's intellectual mentor) who authored the community agitator's handbook "Rules for Radicals" is a complete and total fraud. As Chaput stated,

> "His rules, pressure tactics, deceits, manipulations, and organizing skills are finally based on a fraud. They're not 'progressive' at all. They're the same tired grasping for power that made the world what it is."[48]

I so often want to shake these former students of mine who have become so enamored with their faux-rebellion and pretended progressivism. I want to shout into their souls, "This isn't radical or different...you've become nothing but a conformist acting just like the pattern of this world!" Not that I think it would do much good, but it might make me feel better.

Something that is truly radical is something that goes against the grain of society, something that challenges and upsets the status quo, something that upends the cultural wisdom of the age. You know, something like...the Sermon on the Mount. Saul Alinsky was no radical. He was a conformist who found a way to further the already prevailing philosophies of the world. Jesus of Nazareth was a radical, countering those prevailing philosophies of self-indulgence and decadence with the message of service, self-sacrifice and moral purity.

People who follow Him and His teachings? They are different. They are unique. They are foreigners. They are strangers in a strange land.

In a culture of selfishness, they sacrifice for one another.

In a culture of utilitarianism, they defend the dignity of life made in God's image.

In a culture of moral relativism, they bear witness to God's eternal law.

And they do so in their personal testimony as well as their public action, no matter how much they are criticized, no matter how they are treated, no matter what it may cost them, no matter how *strange* it makes them.

STRANGERS

Not Of, But In

7
THIS LIFE ISN'T YOURS

It's become one of the more popular phrases for Christians to use these days whenever we are frustrated with the direction of our society. Preachers preach it, Sunday School teachers teach it, worship leaders recite it, and congregations are trained to repeat it: "we're in this world, but not of this world."

I think I probably hear the phrase used most often when I'm speaking at or participating in Christian youth events. It's used many times in an effort to get Christian kids to separate themselves from the worldly culture that surrounds them – listen to Christian music instead of hip-hop, don't go to R-rated movies, stay off of inappropriate websites, drop the obsession with social media, speak wholesome words instead of being profane.

Don't misunderstand, all of those goals and objectives are worthwhile, but I'm very concerned about the popularization of this phrase within American Christianity. Not because it lacks Biblical origin. There's no question that there is complete Scriptural validity to the phrase. No, my unease comes in how we are interpreting what Jesus was saying; my trepidation is that we are putting our emphasis and focus on the wrong part of His message and thus unintentionally inverting His instruction. But we'll get to that in a later chapter (13 to be precise). For now, let's start with what He said. In the Gospel of John, the author records Jesus' prayer for His disciples:

> "I have given them your word and the world has hated them, for they are not of the world any more than I am of the world. My prayer is not that you take them out of the world but that you protect them from the evil one. They are not of the world, even as I am not of it. Sanctify them by the truth; your word is truth. As you sent me into the world, I have sent them into the world. For them I sanctify myself, that they too may be truly sanctified."[49]

The first thing to notice is the repeated stress Christ places on the fact that He is "not of" this world and that His disciples (and I think it is fair to conclude application for all time) will not be either. I just wrote six previous chapters on this point, but since Jesus put such emphasis on that fact in this prayer, I think it's worthwhile to reiterate it one more time.

It's clear from His word that our presence as "strangers" in this world is not accidental or unprovoked. It's by design. And not only that, Jesus is accentuating in this prayer that we are to make a conscious effort to *remain* strangers through an act of the will. We are to separate ourselves in thought and action, and refuse to "seek citizenship" in this world. When Titus writes of believers having become "heirs" to God's eternal kingdom through our relationship with Jesus[50], he is underscoring the importance of a complete divorce from the world.

STRANGERS

But what does that mean? Clearly we are still impacted and affected by the worldly events unfolding around us. As much as we might want to disassociate from the suffering, poverty, pain, disasters and tragedies of the world, we cannot. The calamities of our fallen world visit themselves upon believers every bit as much as they do on unbelievers.

What Jesus is talking about is not a physical isolation from the world, but a mental and spiritual liberty from its intractable nature and hopeless destiny. He is alluding to the Biblical truth a Christian acknowledges that once we have signed onto citizenship in heaven, this life on earth is no longer about us or for us. Our lives are not our own. Paul encourages us in this regard when he writes to the Philippians,

> "What is more, I consider everything a loss
> because of the surpassing worth of
> knowing Christ Jesus my Lord, for whose sake I
> have lost all things. I consider them garbage,
> that I may gain Christ and be found in him, not
> having a righteousness of my own that comes
> from the law, but that which is through faith
> in Christ—the righteousness that comes from
> God on the basis of faith...
>
> Not that I have already obtained all this, or
> have already arrived at my goal, but I press on
> to take hold of that for which Christ Jesus took
> hold of me. Brothers and sisters, I do not
> consider myself yet to have taken hold of it. But
> one thing I do: Forgetting what is behind and
> straining toward what is ahead, I press
> on toward the goal to win the prize for which
> God has called me heavenward in Christ
> Jesus."[51]

True Christianity is a mindset that is liberated from the worldly concerns of health, wealth and status. It is a mindset that clings not to the tattered trappings of the earth's fleeting pleasures, but finds contentment in the promised life of everlasting joy yet to come.

Now truthfully, it's easy to write those words but certainly not easy to live them. When you lose your job, your spouse, your child, or when you observe the unjust triumphs of godless men, every believer I've ever known finds it nearly impossible to simply write those things off as "loss" compared to knowing Jesus. I sometimes wonder how much Paul's human nature was warring against the perfect inspiration of the Holy Spirit when he was putting those divine words to paper. But regardless, the degree to which we are able to consign worldly worries to the rank of "garbage" reflects the amount of freedom our soul will find.

That said, there is a dangerous teaching that comes from this mindset that is affecting the church with, as always, the best of intentions. I am aware of it because sadly, I have preached it – and as a result, I have repented for it. In fact, my excessive entanglement with this false teaching was so great that I actually spoke it at a commencement ceremony to a graduating class of high school seniors several years ago. The phrase I uttered was: "Living is biological, but life is spiritual."

Of course there are other iterations of the same concept. We sometimes say things like, "This old shell isn't me. I'm what's on the inside." There's even a popular quote attributed to the great Christian thinker C.S. Lewis that circles the internet and social media repackaging the same philosophy. Perhaps you've seen it (or re-tweeted it) or one of its variations: "I'm not a body that has a soul. I'm a soul that has a body."

C.S. Lewis never said that, and from everything I've ever read of and from him, he would have never believed it. The teaching is steeped in a dangerous gnostic spiritualism that wrests the two (body and soul) apart. It becomes, as one author has put it, an "either/or proposition."[52] You're either an immortal soul or you're a withering old sack of bones. The problem is that isn't Biblical.

Clearly God has created us and given us both physical and spiritual components. So rather than an "either/or" scenario, it's a "both/and" proposition.[53] Remember that from the beginning, God gave Adam a physical body to exist in a state of perfection. It is anti-Biblical to suggest that Adam was merely a spirit in the Garden of Eden before he ate the forbidden fruit. The fact that Eve was taken from his rib indicates explicitly what is implied throughout the Creation account. Physical bodies did not come into existence as a result of sin; physical bodies were always part of God's plan for humans.

It's why God comes to us in both realms. He certainly comes to us in the spiritual world: giving us prayer and intercession, faith, the indwelling of the Holy Spirit, angelic protection and sanctification. But he also interacts with us in the physical world as well, giving us His Word to read and study, baptism to experience, communion to take in remembrance, music and words with which to praise and fellowship, reason and intellect to think and discover.

Saying we are "not of this world" then is not to be understood as a license to disregard the physical. If that were the case, why fight to preserve the well-being of others, or to improve the physical plight of the less fortunate? Why would gluttony be sinful? Why should we be concerned with our own health or with the infant mortality rate or starvation? Why respect and care for the physical body of others or ourselves at all? Why would it matter? If life is not equally physical, why not just end it and get on with the good stuff...the "real" stuff?

No, the phrase "not of this world" is not implying or affirming some hedonistic, libertine view of humanity. As Paul wrote, it's a mindset and outlook that Christians hold – and the more mature we are in our faith, the more we are able to maintain that outlook amidst the inevitable misfortunes of a fallen physical existence. It allows us to properly identify with James' affirmation that our lives are a "mist that appears for a little while and then vanishes."[54] Far from discouraging, that reality drastically refocuses and recalibrates our perspective onto eternal things. It offers a hope that sets us apart in this world. Remember the passage from Peter I cited earlier? Apart from this truly Christian mindset, it would seem so confusing:

> "In all this you greatly rejoice, though now for a little while you may have had to suffer grief in all kinds of trials. These have come so that the proven genuineness of your faith—of greater worth than gold, which perishes even though refined by fire—may result in praise, glory and honor when Jesus Christ is revealed. Though you have not seen him, you love him; and even though you do not see him now, you believe in him and are filled with an inexpressible and glorious joy, for you are receiving the end result of your faith, the salvation of your souls."[55]

But don't limit that amazing belief to just our dying and departing moments – something I believe we do too often. We reduce Christian hope to the funeral home, pointing out how it is what makes a Christian funeral so much more pleasant than the non-Christian. First of all, that isn't entirely accurate. Other faiths offer hope of life-after-death in various forms (Hindu reincarnation being just one example). Secondly, I have attended several Christian funerals that are racked with grief – particularly when young children are involved. Christian hope is not a deliverance from earthly sorrow, and we shouldn't confuse it as such or we do a disservice to Scripture and to those who aren't sure whether to believe in it.

I guess what I'm saying is that Biblically speaking, being "not of this world" is far less about your manner at a gravesite and far more about your daily life, where Christian hope is to manifest itself in undeniable ways.

S╋RANGERS

8
STOP BEING OFFENDED

Scholars down through the ages have asserted the two undeniable, inescapable realities of life: (1) death, (2) taxes. I would submit they missed a third: Peter Heck could do no wrong in the eyes of his Granny. It's as certain and as sure a reality as death or taxes. And I have two annoyed siblings who will gladly attest to that truth.

When I was 10 years old and lathered up my older brother's toothbrush with the muscle relaxer Icy Hot (which smells remarkably like the toothpaste Pepsodent by the way), it was my Granny who rushed to my defense.

As poor Andrew stood in her bathroom cupping handfuls of cold water to douse his flaming gums and tongue (to this day that remains one of the funniest sights I have ever been privileged to witness), and my Mom and Dad began to contemplate my inevitable punishment for the dirty (but hilarious) deed, it was Granny who objected to the iron hand of parental justice about to descend upon me.

"I'm sure he just got confused," turned into, "Oh, he didn't mean to," and finally, "It's probably good for Andrew's teeth and gums anyway." As he listened to Granny's protests against the backdrop of rushing water and his heart pounding through his gums, Andrew's face was priceless.

It's true though; I could have set their house on fire and Granny would have been the first one in the yard toasting marshmallows, bragging to the firemen how no one can build a fire like me.

But besides her tireless defense of my character, motives and overall existence, there is one other thing about my Granny that I will never forget. She had no patience for idiots. In fact, frankly, she was disgusted by them.

Her favorite phrase that I heard emanating from her lips repeatedly as she set crocheting in her rocking chair, watching the nightly news accounts of criminals, thugs and all those who lived in rebellion to God was, "Well I never..."

Now if you're from my Granny's generation, you know that you don't finish that phrase. You don't have to. It stands on its own as a decimation of the galactic ignorance of anyone who would behave in such an obviously absurd manner.

And to be honest, these days it could (if we let it) become the collective motto of American Christians who truly live by the Word of God. Just open your eyes, turn on the TV, engage a neighbor in conversation about religion or politics, listen for just a few moments and I guarantee you will feel the overwhelming desire to let out one of my Granny's patented sighs of disgust and finish with a, "Well I never..."

But don't do it. Don't let yourself do it.

STRANGERS

One of the ways Christian hope is to manifest itself in our lives, one of the ways we are truly to live as ambassadors sent into the world to do a job, is to stop being so offended all the time. I made the decision a few years ago to not live that way.

Being offended is always a personal choice we make, and it's one that actually empowers those with whom we disagree. Giving someone else the power to offend you is surrendering the light we possess, choosing to hide it under a bushel of hurt feelings and fragile sensibilities. Toughen up.

That isn't to say that things we encounter in this world shouldn't shock our conscience. They should and they will unless we become dangerously desensitized to the ungodliness that surrounds us. But people who are perpetually offended are tiresome, obnoxious and largely ineffective. There's nothing pro-active about taking offense.

Several years ago there was a movie that came out called "Dogma" starring a litany of Hollywood elites including Matt Damon and Ben Affleck who were fallen angels banished to Wisconsin, seeking help from Chris Rock (the 13th Disciple) and George Carlin (a corrupt priest) to get back to Heaven. According to every review I read, the film was blasphemous in about every way imaginable.

As a result, I didn't see the movie. But I also didn't participate in the numerous protests demanding the movie be stricken from the theater (an action that sadly had the opposite of its desired affect, creating controversy and intrigue about an otherwise poor attempt at cinematic comedy).

In one interview on ABC's 20/20, an unidentified Catholic woman called for there to be no movies that mocked religion. Any religion. Ever. Her reasoning was simply, "It's too holy, it's our whole salvation."

I felt so bad for this woman who had given the director of

this silly movie the power to offend her so deeply. Seriously, you could see it in her face and hear it in her voice – she was grieved and hurting. She acted as though she might have even believed the debut of this film could potentially strip her of her salvation. I so wanted to find her and tell her that far from being shocked, this flick is precisely what she should be expecting from the world.

The disciples and early Christians faced far worse treatment than a contemptuous film, and yet lived lives of joy, continuing on about their mission refusing to be overpowered by the wiles of foolish men.

Without intending to heap criticism upon this well-intentioned woman, we are not living lives empowered by the same Spirit those disciples and early believers possessed (a Spirit promised to us) if we are daunted and hindered in our mission of joy by ignorant Hollywood plots.

The same goes for caustic Facebook comments, mean-spirited tweets, derogatory memes, taunting YouTube videos and an excess of articles, commentaries and books that mock our beliefs and ridicule our faith.

Who knows what motivates the hearts of those who perpetrate those transgressions against our consciences – it could easily be ignorance, a desire to conform, or insecurity. If I had to bet, I would contend that more often than not, those who feel compelled to attack our faith – or attack us personally *because* of our faith – are doing so for the very reason Romans 1:18 tells us: they are unrighteously suppressing the truth that we all know.

In July of 2016, the Christian apologetics ministry Answers in Genesis opened their world-class theme park built around a life-size replica of Noah's Ark (it is built to match Biblical specifications). In the lead-up to its debut, several atheist groups attempted to deride the project, mocking its creators, its purpose and its usefulness.

Some of my fellow Christians (and if I was guessing, some of the wonderful folks who work at AiG) were really offended by many of the comments and billboards that these "free-thinkers" (there really couldn't be a more accurate term to describe individuals who take pride in having their thoughts and ideas tethered to no reliable foundation or fixed point of reference) put up, accusing the Christians of celebrating genocide and incest.

But why? Why be offended and give these scoffers precisely what they desire?

Why not revel in the attention they are bringing to a godly enterprise?

Why not sarcastically return fire by pointing out these humanists are actually making the Ark experience all the more real by depicting so admirably the mockery and scorn that previous generations of fools heaped upon the real Noah as he built the original vessel?

Why not find humor In the fact that these God-deniers are getting terribly exercised over something they love to pretend isn't real?

After all, I can't imagine spending an ounce of my energy or resources to buy billboards or finance ad campaigns in an attempt to deprogram someone of their belief in Santa Claus or the Easter Bunny. If atheists and humanists don't believe in any supernatural divinity at all, why do they invest so much of their time, money and effort in attacking it? Could it be because they actually know the truth, but they are selfishly "suppressing the truth in unrighteousness" in a desperate and futile effort to hide from the moral accountability that comes with God's existence?

Do you know how much more effective Christians could be

at influencing and impacting the world around us if we didn't act as though we should be immune from criticism? Far too many of us fall into the trap of believing that being "not of" this world means that we must act offended at everything the world does or says. And so we embrace a hypersensitivity that leaves the impression we expect better of godless men.

Why would we? And pray-tell how many of those godless men are likely to be won over or influenced by people who appear so pretentious and entitled that they cry foul the moment their feelings have been hurt?

We long for the opportunity to impact the world we've been sent into, but we derail those opportunities time and time again with our offended egos. As nationally syndicated radio host Hugh Hewitt explains,

> "Very successful people have little time for those with long lists of grievances, real or imagined, but especially for those that are imagined."[56]

Think about this. If anyone had a right to be *constantly* offended, would it not have been Jesus Himself? The One through whom all things had been made walking the corrupted earth that He had designed perfect, walking among the proud and sinful beings He had created for humble worship and relationship, enduring the most humiliating of treatments in the most lowly of circumstances in the most hostile of environments.

And yet, outside of the desecration of His Father's temple, it would be nearly impossible to pinpoint any moment in the ministry of Christ where you could accurately peg Him as "offended." If Jesus found a way to avoid the temptation of being perpetually offended, surely we must make the effort too.

That's not saying it will be easy. If you don't celebrate

Christmas with trees and Santa Claus, you will be tempted to take offense at those who do.

If you despise *Harry Potter* books, you will be tempted to take offense at those who don't.

If you think Christian rap or Christian metal is an entrance ramp onto the Highway to Hell, you will be tempted to take offense by those who dig them.

If you believe that the government (public) school system is debased beyond repair, you will be tempted to take offense towards those who use it and defend it.

If you abstain from alcohol, tobacco and tattoos because you see them as an affront to the temple of God that is your body, you will be tempted to take offense at the hoards of tatted-up casual drinking smokers that surround you.

If you are able to keep your tongue in check and express yourself without the use of profanity, you will be tempted to take offense at the increasing flock of potty mouths.

Don't. No matter how easy it would be. Remember the Christian life was never intended to be easy. You are a stranger. Things are rarely easy for strangers in a foreign land. So in the immortal words of my 7th grade football coach who got fired for telling us we needed to trade in our shoulder pads for a bunch of bras, "suck it up, buttercup."

That said, please understand, none of this means that you are to roll over in the face of conflict. Please don't misinterpret my words to suggest that a Christian is to be a doormat for the world. That couldn't be further from the truth. The point I'm making in this chapter is to say that when inevitable conflict with the world comes (and it will come), don't react by empowering your enemy by taking offense.

Instead choose to respond in a way that honors God and

strengthens your effectiveness.

9
BE COOL WITH BEING UNCOOL

Sometime in the middle of July 2015 after the U.S. Supreme Court rewrote centuries of law and mandated "gay marriage" on the country, I woke up to the sound of my cell phone ringing on the other side of the room. When I finally stumbled my way over to it, I had missed the incoming call but noticed that I had a message waiting on me from a minister friend of mine. Though we get along well, he isn't someone who would normally be calling me just to chat – especially early in the morning. So somewhat concerned as much as curious, I listened to his voicemail that pretty much said, "Check your email as soon as you can. Hope you're doing well."

With my interest peaked, I got out the laptop and logged in to read this email:

9 BE COOL WITH BEING UNCOOL

Hi Peter,

If you have a chance, could you look at the statement [regarding the church's position on the Supreme Court's gay marriage decree] I posted on our church FB page and give me your thoughts? Did I misrepresent, set myself up, or miss the point? I am certainly not an expert on these matters but felt my congregation needed to hear something from me. It has been received well but then was attacked pretty hard by a couple of LGBT sympathizers yesterday and so I responded to them as well. Please feel free to weigh in.

When I went to the page, I saw the sympathizers he was speaking about were engaged in typical trolling – posting offensive rhetoric and taunting comments to chide believers over their recent "loss" in the high court of Washington, D.C.

First and foremost, let me stress this point a million times over: Christians never truly lose unless they fail to honor God and remain faithful to Him. Salvation in Christ has brought us the eternal victory that nothing can overturn. No matter what man may do or say, no matter what he may pretend or what he may legalize or litigate in this temporary life, a Christian cannot and will not fail if he honors God.

If Christians would grasp this simple point that God has not called us to "win" anything here on earth, but rather faithfully serve Him no matter the cost to us personally, we would not only relieve ourselves of inordinate amounts of undue, unintended pressures and stress, but we would also heap burning coals on the heads of our enemies.

This is a principle that is understood even in children's books. When the Grinch steals all your presents and food, you can still join hands with every Who down in Whoville and express gratitude. And what does it do to your enemy? Deprives him of his victory, annoys him to no end, and maybe – just maybe – causes his heart to grow a few sizes.

And perusing this particular church's Facebook page that morning, it was clear that a slew of cultural Grinches had descended upon them. The kind of reaction they were producing was strategic and intentional. From the beginning of the sexual revolution, the objective of the ungodly has been to attack the church and Christianity as hypocritical, judgmental and obsolete. After all, nothing else besides the unchanging and absolute Judeo-Christian moral ethic stands in the way of the godless objective of social sexual anarchy. This is precisely why gay activist authors Marshall Kirk and Hunter Madsen wrote in their infamous 1989 blueprint for the homosexualization of America, *After the Ball*:

> "[P]ropagandistic advertisement can depict homophobic and homohating bigots as crude loudmouths...who are 'not Christian.'"[57]

And that was exactly the tenor of the comments I was reading on my computer screen. "No church who really loved God would stand against equality." "No Christian who serves Jesus would want to deprive another one of God's children of their happiness." "Who would Jesus hate?" And on and on and on.

One commenter had even gone to the trouble of posting a very popular video from gay activist Matt Baume where he attempted to dismantle the notion of "traditional marriage." Baume has become a sort of cult hero on the American political left, writing and recording pieces like this that mock Christians in humanist publications like the *Huffington Post*:

> "Traditional marriage isn't exactly the 'one man, one woman' story you've always heard. Politicians may claim that the definition of

73

marriage hasn't changed in thousands of years, but it most definitely has. Marriage has been through a lot of changes over the millennia — most good, some bad.

For example, in Mesopotamia of 4,000 years ago, marriage was similar to slavery. The laws even included the rules for getting a refund if you weren't satisfied with your wife.

Romans found public displays of affection offensive, and one senator had to resign after he was seen kissing his wife in public. Early church officials discouraged people from marrying altogether, since it distracted them from praying. And a thousand years ago, girls were married when their ages were still in the single-digits.

For a long time, marriage was a lousy deal for women. Bernard of Siena told his male parishioners that they should show their wives as much mercy as they would a pig, and even Martin Luther said that he hit his wife for being 'saucy.'"[58]

And so it went. The video version continues harpooning all the various eccentricities and errors of judgment made in marital relationships down through the ages, apparently attempting to convince the viewer that, "People have been jacking up marriage for millennia, so why not let the gays have a crack at it?" Now that's intellectualism if I've ever heard it.

But of course, emotionalism, not intellectualism, is the preferred appeal here. For those who are capable of thinking, this Baume video and commentary is a train wreck almost from beginning to end. Baume may have carved out a reputation as stylistically polished, but the video quite unintentionally stands as a devastating dismantling of the perversions, distortions and corruptions that man has cast upon the divine institution of marriage down through the ages.

In other words, fast forward fifty years or so, and we could create the same video, except add to his litany of "marriage redefinitions" the preposterous invention of so-called same-sex "marriage" as yet another example of the ways in which man has abused the marital covenant established in Genesis. Far from being vindication for acceptance of "gay marriage," Baume's video provides great reason to oppose it!

Keep in mind one other particularly peculiar and hilarious part of Baume's literary and videographic efforts. Throughout his entire rant chronicling the marital relationship throughout world history, *each and every example* he gives actually references the union of man and woman. He mocks various characteristics about it, or points out error in the manner those relationships have been accepted or approved. But while supposedly attempting to set forth the idea that the tradition of man/woman marriage is a farce, he can point only to the tradition of man/woman marriage in history. Oops.

Granted, he does make valid points about the wrong-headed assessments, interpretations, and rules governing the institution that fallen men have placed on it. But ironically each of those mistakes would be properly characterized as being Biblically unjustifiable. God and His word didn't get it wrong. Man did. So Baume's grand idea? Forget God's design and follow man's. See why I said emotionalism, not intellectualism, is what drives this drivel?

So how should a Christian respond to this kind of nonsense? Not by being offended that someone has dared to attack God's word (see previous chapter), but by demonstrating how foolish it is to do so. That's exactly what I did when I weighed in on that Facebook page. I pointed out that I could make the same video of Baume, using the exact same examples he gave, but adding to it the newly initiated so-called "gay marriage" (including all the pathetic attempts to justify its existence in Scripture). And I could drive it home to this point: when we abandon what God designed in the Garden of Eden... a loving, selfless, sacrificial and servant-oriented relationship and partnership between man and woman... we really screw things up. Whether it's racial expectations, polygamous unions, slave-oriented couplings, abusive treatment, or same-sex relationships, they all are an affront to what God intended, and therefore are a blight on our human experience.

The anti-Christian LGBT sympathizer who had posted the video responded to my comment by writing back, "Whatever. This is Facebook, not an academic lecture." Burning coals. This is precisely how we should be engaging the hostile nature of the ungodly around us. Not by taking offense, and not by doing what far too many believers do these days – running away or cowering behind transparent dodges like, "we just want to love everybody." No, we should be standing firm on the Word of God and demonstrating that we are resilient and undaunted.

After all, these types of cultural assaults on the authority of God and the Bible are nothing new. Not even in America. I was fascinated by reading a piece by the Gospel Coalition's Trevin Wax recently where he compared current attacks on the church's sexual ethics to previous attacks on the church's scientific literacy a century ago.

Whereas today those that oppose the sexual permissiveness of the culture and its normalization of depravity are met with charges of weakening the church by prudish irrelevance, in the early 1900s those that clung to the authority of miraculous supernatural events recorded in Scripture were charged with weakening the church by denying science. Wax writes,

"Many church leaders sought to distinguish the kernel of Christianity (the fatherhood of God and brotherhood of man) from the shell of Christianity (miracle stories that came from another cultural vantage point). One could still maintain the moral center of Christianity while disregarding the events that required suspension of disbelief.

As this adaptation spread, belief in the bodily resurrection of Jesus was reinterpreted and given a solely spiritual meaning (he is alive in the hearts of good people). Miracle stories such as Jesus' feeding the 5,000 were given a moral twist (the true miracle is that suddenly everyone shared). The Virgin Birth was rejected altogether."[59]

It was the Presbyterian theologian J. Gresham Machen, Wax noted, that pointed out the obvious: what was taking shape wasn't Christianity at all – it was a humanistic religion wearing a Christian label. And in Christian churches outside the bubble of the West (the "West" meaning North America and western Europe), the reaction to this ungodly movement of cultural compromise was utter shock and dismay.

That's precisely what we see unfolding today with churches that choose, for the sake of cultural relevance, to abandon the Bible's instruction on sexual morality. Call it what you will, it's not Christianity if it rejects the plain teaching of Scripture. And the Christian churches in the Middle East, Asia, South America and Africa are watching Christian abandonment of truth in the United States with disgust. Wax admonishes,

"Churches (in America) that accept society's dogma on marriage and sexuality may think of themselves as "affirming," but the global church sees them as 'apostate.' Meanwhile, it is the height of imperialistic narrowness for a rapidly shrinking subset of white churches in the West to lecture the rest of the world – including those places where Christianity is exploding in growth or where Christians are being martyred – on why they are wrong and how everyone else in Christian history has misread Scripture regarding the meaning of marriage."[60]

It really is remarkable, isn't it? The global church is suffering for their faith in God's Word, while many in the American church are perverting and editing God's Word to appease and affirm sinful man. How will that end? It's pretty easy to find the collected works of theologians like Machen and G.K. Chesterton from the 1900s. Despite being mocked incessantly in their day for their dogged devotion to the "absurdities" of Scripture and reliability of the full text, their words remain while Wax notes the, "names of most of their once-fashionable opponents are largely unrecognizable."[61]

I would contend to Christians tempted to pursue some fleeting cultural recognition and fame by forsaking their allegiance to the full, unadulterated Word of the Living God today, you are making the gravest of mistakes. So what if men call you backwards? Who cares if the godless label you irrelevant and a fool? If you are to be a stranger, should you appear any other way to them?

God has not promised to bring us all to earthly palaces for service as he did for Joseph, Daniel, and Esther. He has merely promised us the opportunity to serve. And the history of man inside and outside the pages of Scripture bear witness to the truth that those who He uses most powerfully are servants who offer more to the world around them than a mere echo of the times.

You have been sent into a hostile world not to concede and compromise in an effort to be cool, but to remain resilient and undaunted in an effort to be faithful.

10
LET YOUR ANGER BE RIGHTEOUS

I understand that as a person grows in their faith, we become more cognizant and aware of our own shortcomings and failures. That doesn't make it any more pleasant to deal with, however. While I'm glad to know I may be maturing in my Christian walk, I could do without the sense of conviction I feel whenever I read Jesus:

> (1) Lecturing the Pharisees who cared more about appearing righteous than they did about living righteously;

> (2) Ripping the Sadducees who were more concerned with their cultural luxuries and prosperity than they were helping hurting people find spiritual rebirth;

(3) Rebuking the Sons of Thunder (James and John) for their desire to pull an Elijah and call down fire from heaven to obliterate Samaria for their insolence.

I know I have been, and too often remain, each of those characters. My preference for tradition leads me too often to behave like a Pharisee. My desire for comfort and leisure leads me too often to behave like a Sadducee. And as for the Sons of Thunder? I think that may be my biggest cross to bear.

When I first started my radio show years ago, I would regularly listen to each program after it aired. Not because I had a massive ego problem (though I'm not discounting it as a possibility), but because I wanted to improve and eliminate verbal tics and habits that annoy listeners. And in those notebooks of self-critique that I took, there was one comment that surfaced repeatedly: "You sound too angry." I remember my Mom telling me that from time to time as well. "Passion is a good thing," she would remind me, "but you can't be angry for two hours and expect people to enjoy your show."

And she was right, of course. I found when I would listen back that I was so passionate about what I was discussing that I would drift from a tone of instruction or debate into a tone of schoolmarm-like condescension that smacked of arrogance and bitterness. That's not productive for holding a radio audience, nor is it productive for influencing the world.

I'm not a preacher by trade, but I have done quite a bit of pulpit-filling over the years and have had to re-learn that same lesson for the church environment as well. To be honest, I am not interested in fluffy, pacifist, "Jesus-is-my-boyfriend" Christianity. Never have been. While I certainly agree that any representation of God that lacks His all-loving, all-caring, omni-benevolent nature is incomplete, I don't think our culture is lacking in that regard. On the contrary, I think the loving grandpa side of God is virtually the only perspective of His

STRANGERS

character that is represented and acknowledged in most American churches these days.

And that drives me nuts. Because if we are misrepresenting God by leaving out his loving nature (which we certainly are), then we are unquestionably misrepresenting God by pretending that's all He is. And so in a semi-conscious corrective effort, most of my messages are geared toward reminding the faithful of the necessary fear of God. Now, I haven't gone full Jonathan Edwards' "Sinners in the Hands of an Angry God" yet. I stress yet, because I think I could deliver this passage from that sermon with impressive flare:

> "The bow of God's wrath is bent, and the arrow made ready on the string, and justice bends the arrow at your heart, and strains the bow, and it is nothing but the mere pleasure of God, and that of an angry God, without any promise or obligation at all, that keeps the arrow one moment from being made drunk with your blood... Unconverted men walk over the pit of hell on a rotten covering."[62]

A bow and arrow prop, sound effects of a man falling through a rotted out floorboard, perfectly timed pyrotechnics and I think my modernized version of this classic could be a sermon for the ages. But all joking aside, there is nothing unbiblical about tempering your messages with meekness, humility and effectively restrained strength. None of those things diminish passion or truth. They can, however, make you more effective in the world you've been sent into.

Remember, people who are perpetually angry become known as hotheads and are rarely, if ever, taken seriously. They become comical figures that no one respects, but everyone chides behind their back, complete with red-face tomato memes sent around the office or eye rolls and head nods when another eruption is happening across the room.

I'm thankful because my nature is not that of an angry person at all. My wife and I don't really fight, and when we do it's bickering – I cannot remember a time when I have been legitimately angry with her. The same goes for my children. They have annoyed or frustrated me to the point of wanting to throw myself through the front window, but I can't remember ever feeling genuine anger. I imagine a lot of that comes from my Dad's example. He's always been an easygoing guy with no blood pressure problems. Of course, the genetic side is also aided by his commitment to God's Word and the discipline of self-control taught by the Holy Spirit. But suffice it to say that I'm thankful for his example, whatever the major cause of his even temperament may be.

When I was writing this chapter I turned and asked Jenny, "Can you remember a time when I was really angry?" She sat and thought about it, and we both ended up laughing about some silly arguments we got into, particularly early in our marriage. But in the end, she concluded that no, she doesn't think she has ever seen me angry. Now, I'm not saying all of this to brag, primarily because I'm not convinced there is anything there to brag about. It's not that I care to debate whether anger is a good or bad thing, but that Biblically I think it's important to remember there is an appropriate place for it. Jesus got angry, after all. But there are a couple important lessons we can take from those overturned money-changers tables as we are sent into this world as His ambassadors.

First, His was a righteous anger that didn't cross over into sinful rage or thoughtless wrath. And secondly, everyone remembers this event because it was so out of the ordinary. Jesus never flew off the handle, and so when He displayed righteous anger, He gained the attention of those around Him. His anger was a tool, harnessed and used perfectly to engender the type of response He desired.

Don't forget that Jesus had taught respect for His Father's house throughout His entire ministry. He taught reverence, and to render unto God what belongs to Him – admiration, respect, worship and honor. Those calm and reasoned teachings had apparently fallen on deaf ears when it came to the hacks selling chicken eggs on the table of consecrated bread. And so Jesus got His point across.

The Bible doesn't say for sure, but I would think it's a fairly safe assumption to suggest that the traveling carnival barkers picked up shop and moved to the streets after that scene. To influence the world you've been sent into, strive to use anger for righteous reasons only, and very infrequently at that. Don't become someone known for his or her anger. Become known as someone who understands its proper use.

There's non-biblical evidence for the soundness of this advice as well. Ronald Reagan was unquestionably the greatest president of my lifetime. Known for his warm smile and genial personality, Reagan was as quick with a joke as any chief executive the country has ever seen. Unlike President Bill Clinton who became notorious for his frequent and comical fits of rage, Reagan was as even-keeled as you can imagine for someone under such pressure. And therefore, when times like this occurred, it had a lasting impact:

> "In the middle of a debate between candidates for the presidency that had been organized by his campaign, Ronald Reagan once famously announced, 'I paid for that microphone.' He showed a flash of anger that contrasted with his geniality. That is the perfect contradiction: a reputation for good humor and a ready laugh are the frame in which flashing anger is always best displayed. Don't bother with the anger until you have built the frame."[63]

Christians are not to shy away from conflict. The contemporary rewriting of Jesus to fit the mold of some new age hipster who preached some pre-Woodstock version of hippie "peace and love" is downright heresy. Jesus was as blunt and as confrontational as any figure you can find throughout history. I recently challenged some young people to a game of "Who Said It?" I put a quote up on the screen and gave them choices as to who uttered the famous words. Some of them were fun, some were serious, but all of them were largely guessed correctly except this one:

> "Do not think that I came to bring peace on earth. I did not come to bring peace but a sword."[64]

When I told those high school students that the quote was taken right from the red letters in Matthew 10, they seemed shocked. When I explained the context of the verse it sank in and made sense to them, but I think it's important to consider why it may have seemed so bizarre to them that Jesus could have said those words.

First, and most likely, because we are misrepresenting Jesus in our culture, allowing His blunt and divisive ministry to be hijacked by those who want a New Age Jesus to put on their dashboards and relegate to a mere moral philosopher. But the other reason this phrase sounded so "un-Jesus-like" is worth noting. We equate division with vitriol and anger. But Jesus was not an angry fellow. So how could someone divide without being known as an angry little cuss? Because He harnessed and restrained His emotions perfectly, understanding the message was more vital than the passion.

When the message is best advanced through quiet whispers and silent prayers, use them. When it is best advanced through impassioned debate or serious discussion, use them. When it is best advanced through humor and sarcastic wit, use them. And yes, when it is best advanced through flashes of righteous anger and a fighting spirit, use them.

11
FRIENDLY TO ALL, FRIENDS
WITH THE SELECT

I started writing this chapter in the middle of the school year, and it actually inspired me to do something to one of my classes. When the bell rang, I stood up and told the class to get out a half sheet of paper. The inevitable groans and moans came from nearly every seat, and some verbally objected that, "You didn't tell us there was going to be a quiz." The concept of pop quizzes is apparently foreign these days.

But this wasn't going to be a typical quiz anyway. I had them number to five and proceeded to ask four fairly mundane, general and easy questions regarding the topic we were currently studying. Then I got to number five.

Me: Number five. Write down the name of one of the two guys who cleans these rooms every night.

Confused student 1: Wait what?

Me: Write down the name of one of the two guys who cleans these rooms every night.

Confused student 2: I don't understand. You mean the janitors?

Me: Yes, or the custodians, whichever term you prefer.

Confused student 3: Why are you asking this?

Confused student 4: What does this have anything to do with what we're studying?

Me: Oh, it doesn't necessarily.

Confused student 5: So why would you ask us something that we're not studying?

Me: Because it's something you should know anyway.

Confused student 6: Why? Why should we know somebody we've never talked to?

Me: Well that's just it. You really shouldn't if you've never talked to them. But the point is that maybe you should be talking to them. You rely on them more than you know. And in life you're gonna meet all kinds of people, every single one being just as valuable and significant as you. So start by introducing yourself.

Confused student 7: This is stupid.

To be honest, maybe confused student 7 was right. Maybe

it was stupid. Maybe I was trying or straining too hard to make a point. In the end, I made the quiz worth 4 points instead of 5, and gave extra credit to anyone who got the janitor question right (which some of them did). I wanted to avoid the rage of the class valedictorian's parents if he lost his number one ranking because of that question.

But I still think the exercise was useful, and I'm hopeful that it will at least be something they think about the next time they pass one of the janitors in the hallway. The whole thing started to be very personally convicting when I considered whether or not I would pass my own quiz. I know the two guys who clean the rooms, but what about all the receptionists where I work, the security personnel, the cafeteria workers? Could you pass the quiz?

We talk about the word "kindness" all the time and use it to label people we barely even know. "They seem nice" or "they're a nice person" become generalized labels we just slap onto individuals regardless of the true content of their character. Truthfully, it's pretty easy to pass the world's kindness test. It pretty much comes down to this: do you hurt people intentionally? If so, you're not kind. If not, congratulations, you're officially "nice."

And by the way, there's actually a loophole worked into the worldly standards that you can effectively exploit. If the person in question is being a jerk to you (or has been at some point – no statute of limitations), you can tell them off and get a kindness pass. I know I don't have to belabor this point because you're either guilty of it, or you've seen it perpetrated by fellow Christians.

There are believers who will regularly use the truths we've just discussed (Christians are not to be doormats for the culture, Jesus was a divisive person, there is a time for righteous anger) to justify or rationalize their desire to trash another person's reputation.

To be blunt and honest, this is sometimes a struggle for me that I have to guard against. With the nature of what I do, it is a dangerous temptation I face regularly to intentionally blur the line between obliterating bad ideas and obliterating people who voice those bad ideas. I will take the chiding, the irritation, the derision and foolishness for a time, but then I will let loose. Whether it's in print, behind a microphone, or online through social media, I far too often indulge the corrupt human side of me that mistakes my enemy (Satan) with his captives (my critics).

Falling into the trap, I'm quick to justify (or attempt to) with the best of them: "I'm defending God's people from being impugned" or "I'm defending God's Word from ridicule" or "I'm defending the defenseless from attack." And I can roll out an impressive array of Bible verses to back it up and sound persuasive. And to make matters worse, there is usually a healthy group of fellow believers who desperately want me to put some of these obnoxious tormenters in their place. So rather than hold me accountable privately, they cheer me on. (Please notice how I am now attempting to prove my sin is your fault...I told you I'm good at this).

But the truth is a Christian's influence in the world will not be expanded or strengthened by trashing the reputation or character of others. That's true for me in my spheres of influence, and it's true for you in yours. Mocking a coworker with your colleagues or talking bad about them behind their backs at the water cooler is no less offensive to God's expectations than my acerbic pen in the newspaper.

Scripture counsels us that personal rebuke and complaint is to be handled privately whenever possible and that we are to treat the offender with charity. Remember what Jesus taught:

> "If you love only those who love you, what
> reward is there for that? Even corrupt tax
> collectors do that much. If you are kind only to

your friends, how are you different from anyone else? Even pagans do that."[65]

If we want to impact the world we've been sent into, we have to do better. C.S. Lewis wrote,

"There are no ordinary people. You have never talked to a mere mortal."[66]

What does he mean? He means every single being you encounter has a role to play in God's eternal story. Every person you see, regardless of the importance assigned to them by this world, has all the meaning and value that you possess. And if God places eternal significance on them, surely it isn't too much to ask for His followers to do the same.

This kind of action – extending to every being made in God's image the dignity with which He has endowed them – is a profound way of separating yourself from the ways of the world. And it can have immediate and long-lasting impacts in ways you wouldn't imagine.

Without revealing names or many details, I can provide an example of this very reality. Not long ago I was embroiled in a controversy (shocker, I know) that made its way into the newspapers. I granted an interview to one particular outlet that I later found out was completely hostile to my position. In fact, they were working on a sneak attack against me by planning to do some creative editing, all to weaken my position publicly. At their editorial meeting I was being mocked and ridiculed pretty severely when a young woman spoke up. She said (according to two sources who were present), "I happen to know Mr. Heck personally. I know he is a kind and good person who doesn't deserve to be treated like this. Think what you want of his ideas and beliefs. But be fair to this man and do your jobs the right way or I'm done."

The five other editors in the room immediately apologized

and carried out very fair and impartial coverage from that point forward. The young woman who had stood up for me was someone I had known five or six years earlier. I had taken the initiative to forge a relationship and friendship with her. And now years later, with no ongoing connection to my ministry work or me, she remembered my kindness towards her and changed the entire media template of that paper. And the story gets better: I know what happened in that room because I was told by two of the editors who eventually came around to my side of the issue and reached out to me. Not only did she pull my reputation from the fire amongst her peers, but she put two of them on the path of reconciliation with the Scriptural position I was taking. All because of kindness.

Your most lasting impact on earth may well come in a time and place you don't even realize. Don't miss it. Forge relationships. Now, there's an important word of warning from Scripture when it comes to those relationships. Peter cautions,

> "Dear friends, I urge you, as foreigners and exiles, to abstain from sinful desires, which wage war against your soul. Live such good lives among the pagans that, though they accuse you of doing wrong, they may see your good deeds and glorify God on the day he visits us."[67]

The second verse of that passage reemphasizes what I was just talking about – treat others with such genuine kindness that when your enemies accuse you of all sorts of evil, no one will believe it. But the first verse is important to notice as well. If, as foreigners and exiles (another way of saying strangers), we are to abstain from sinful desires, we must remember that "friendliness" does not equate Biblically to "friendship." In other words, while we are to be friendly to everyone, we must be very cautious about the friendships that we forge.

The Apostle Paul explained the critical reason why this is

the case when he wrote to the Corinthian church that, "Bad company corrupts good character."[68] In the larger context of the passage it is clear that Paul is warning against the false teachers in Corinth who were arguing that the resurrection of Christ was a myth. These false teachers represented a clear danger to the faith of many believers, and so Paul was advising them not to even associate with these men lest they be misled.

But what Paul most likely thought was a timely message for an individual situation at that local church, the Holy Spirit clearly saw as a timeless lesson for future generations of believers. The apologetics ministry *GotQuestions* summarizes it this way:

> "The point Paul makes here is pertinent to all people in all ages. When we associate with or take delight in the company of people with worldly morals, we run the risk of mimicking their behaviors, their language, and their habits. Before long we are no longer of Christ, but of the world with its denial of absolute authority, its rejection of the Bible as the Word of God, and its ideology of relative morality."[69]

It's one of the gravest mistakes that Christian parents make. When their children begin to befriend and associate with ungodly classmates, well-intentioned parents begin viewing their children's role as that of missionary. "Maybe God has placed these ungodly, screwed up kids in my child's life so that they can be witnessed to," they repeat. Yes, maybe. Or maybe Satan has placed these ungodly, screwed up kids there, which is why God has placed you in your child's life to protect them? Mission friendships end up working out about as well as mission dating ("I know my boyfriend isn't a Christian, but I will date him to convert him"). The ungodly have a key advantage in the battle over who converts whom. It's called human nature.

Time and again in Scripture, God's people (those who are

"slaves to Christ"[70]) are warned that the wise will not intermingle with the ungodly pagans (those who are "slaves to sin"[71]):

> "The righteous should choose his friends carefully, for the way of the wicked leads them astray."[72]

> "Do not be yoked together with unbelievers. For what do righteousness and wickedness have in common?"[73]

> "A companion of fools suffers harm."[74]

> "Stay away from a fool."[75]

> "Do not make friends with a hot-tempered person, do not associate with one easily angered."[76]

Now notice that none of that instruction encourages us to mistreat unbelievers. It is meant as a protective path for the wise to guard against the influence of those who would lead us down the path of destruction. In our depraved culture, that would be a lesson worth learning.

To revisit the theme from the earliest chapters, avoiding the snares of the godless does not mean retreating to lives of hermits and loners. When Christ sends us into the world He intends for us to have relationship with that world. It's the nature of the relationship that is in question. Clearly from the counsel of Scripture, it is to be friendly but not intimate. And most importantly, it is to be solely for the purpose of evangelism, not mere fraternity.

Everything we do as Christians is to have the ultimate purpose of glorifying God. Do your friendships work towards that end?

12
BE DANIEL

So what happens when you put all these principles we've discussed in the last few chapters together? What does a "stranger" who is "not of this world" look like in practice? In a name? Daniel.

Despite the dumbing down of American Christianity, most believers are at least peripherally familiar with the Old Testament Hebrew Daniel and his overnight lock-in with a pack of hungry lions. But before that popular account, the book of Daniel reveals some very significant lessons for us on God's expectations for His chosen people living at odds with the culture around them.

Let's set the stage: Daniel was about as faithful a follower of God as you can imagine. His prayer life was impeccable, his wisdom authentic, his thirst for righteousness unparalleled in his day. Needless to say, he was far more devout and faithful in his faith than many of us are in our own. And then, in the midst of his faithfulness, his world is rocked by an unplanned, unforeseen, uninvited calamity:

> "In the third year of the reign of Jehoiakim king of Judah, Nebuchadnezzar king of Babylon came to Jerusalem and besieged it. And the Lord delivered Jehoiakim king of Judah into his hand...
>
> Then the king ordered Ashpenaz, chief of his court officials, to bring into the king's service some of the Israelites from the royal family and the nobility— young men without any physical defect, handsome, showing aptitude for every kind of learning, well informed, quick to understand, and qualified to serve in the king's palace. He was to teach them the language and literature of the Babylonians. The king assigned them a daily amount of food and wine from the king's table. They were to be trained for three years, and after that they were to enter the king's service. Among those who were chosen were some from Judah: Daniel, Hananiah, Mishael and Azariah."[77]

Now the Bible doesn't go into excruciating detail here, so it's helpful to rely on extra-biblical history to fully understand what Daniel and his friends endured. Everything we can surmise about Nebuchadnezzar and the Babylonians tell us that in all likelihood Daniel watched his family be killed, and more than likely was subjected to castration. When the Babylonians pillaged, this was standard protocol, leaving us little reason to believe that Daniel and his brethren escaped such a fate.

I understand that we American Christians can get rightfully upset at the circumstances unfolding around us. We lament the loss of religious liberty, and we should. We are outraged at the normalization of perversion, and that's understandable. We are livid at the indoctrination of our children, and that's with good cause. But to this point, none of us have faced the type of cultural collapse that Daniel experienced. So it's very instructive to look to him as an example for how we should be reacting to the challenges facing us. We may feel righteously indignant about our circumstances, but if anyone had a better reason to retaliate against his conditions, it was Daniel. And here's how he responded:

> "But Daniel resolved not to defile himself with the royal food and wine, and he asked the chief official for permission not to defile himself this way. Now God had caused the official to show favor and compassion to Daniel, but the official told Daniel, 'I am afraid of my lord the king, who has assigned your food and drink. Why should he see you looking worse than the other young men your age? The king would then have my head because of you.'
>
> Daniel then said to the guard whom the chief official had appointed over Daniel, Hananiah, Mishael and Azariah, 'Please test your servants for ten days: Give us nothing but vegetables to eat and water to drink. Then compare our appearance with that of the young men who eat the royal food, and treat your servants in accordance with what you see.' So he agreed to this and tested them for ten days."[78]

King Nebuchadnezzar was not content with destroying Jerusalem and its people. He was intent on taking the best and the brightest Jews and indoctrinating them into his ungodly culture. The things they were to learn were to be the ways of Babylon, not the ways of God. The things they were to eat were to be the choicest meats of the King, even if they had been defiled and prohibited by God. The ways they were to indulge pleasure were to be in accordance with Babylonian culture, even if such conduct had been forbidden by God.

Even their names were to be changed. After Nebuchadnezzar had removed them from Jerusalem, look at what he does:

> "The chief official gave them new names: to Daniel, the name Belteshazzar; to Hananiah, Shadrach; to Mishael, Meshach; and to Azariah, Abednego."[79]

Each of those original Jewish names contained a reference to one of the Hebrew names for God. The "el" in both Daniel and Mishael were a tribute to the name Elohim; while the "ah" in both Hananiah and Azariah were a tribute to the name Yahweh. Nebuchadnezzar was attempting nothing short of a comprehensive deletion of these four men's identity in God. Everything about them was to be wiped clean and reanimated by Babylonian culture.

Does this sound familiar? It should. In our schools and universities we are seeing Christians fall prey to the religions and new age philosophies of man at an alarming rate.

God's law has been all but expunged from the public square.

Christians are seduced by temptation to the point there is nothing that distinguishes them from the world.

Churches tailor their messages to merely encourage the "seeker-sensitive" masses, for fear of giving any offense.

Sexual purity is almost as obscure within American Christendom as it is without. The messages emanating from Christians' television screens, earbuds, and even mouths, paint a picture of hearts and minds completely captive to the spirit of the age.

STRANGERS

Unlike Daniel, too many of us have chosen to defile ourselves with the king's royal food. Unlike Daniel, we don't want to potentially stand out by eating merely vegetables and water, so we rationalize our disobedience. We say things like, "You can't possibly change society if you isolate yourself!" But of course this isn't about isolating. Daniel wasn't isolated; he was faithful. This is about taking our cues for behavior from Christ, not the culture. And for those who suggest it won't work, let's return for a moment to Babylon:

> "At the end of the ten days they looked healthier and better nourished than any of the young men who ate the royal food. So the guard took away their choice food and the wine they were to drink and gave them vegetables instead.
>
> To these four young men God gave knowledge and understanding of all kinds of literature and learning. And Daniel could understand visions and dreams of all kinds.
>
> At the end of the time set by the king to bring them into his service, the chief official presented them to Nebuchadnezzar. The king talked with them, and he found none equal to Daniel, Hananiah, Mishael and Azariah; so they entered the king's service. In every matter of wisdom and understanding about which the king questioned them, he found them ten times better than all the magicians and enchanters in his whole kingdom."[80]

Did you catch that? When King Nebuchadnezzar needed advice, who did he end up turning to? The guys who wouldn't conform their behavior or thinking to the culture in order to "fit in." Contrary to the prevailing philosophy of the American church that says we must become more like the world in order to influence it, the testimony of Daniel, Hananiah, Mishael and Azariah teaches us the precise opposite.

When we refuse to conform our thinking and behavior to the standards of society, when we set ourselves apart, when we don't defile ourselves, when we don't act like everyone else, when we choose to listen to God and His word over man and the popular wisdom of our age...we will have *greater* ability to shift the culture and change the world. If you want to have a lasting impact, obey God and not society.

Of course Daniel's fulfillment of these very "stranger" qualities we are wanting to emulate doesn't end there. Notice how just two chapters later, the importance of having faithful friends makes all the difference for these tested believers.

> "King Nebuchadnezzar made an image of gold, sixty cubits high and six cubits wide, and set it up on the plain of Dura in the province of Babylon. He then summoned the satraps, prefects, governors, advisers, treasurers, judges, magistrates and all the other provincial officials to come to the dedication of the image he had set up.
>
> Then the herald loudly proclaimed, 'Nations and peoples of every language, this is what you are commanded to do: As soon as you hear the sound of the horn, flute, zither, lyre, harp, pipe and all kinds of music, you must fall down and worship the image of gold that King Nebuchadnezzar has set up. Whoever does not fall down and worship will immediately be thrown into a blazing furnace.'"[81]

Imagine that scene for just a moment. All these exiled Jews standing on the plain of Dura along with men and women of other faiths living under the reign of Nebuchadnezzar in his sprawling kingdom. The horn sounds and for a split second everyone stands there not knowing if they should bow. Then one does, and a domino effect ensues. You can even hear their excuses: "We don't really want to do this, but God would want us to live," or "God knows the truth in our hearts that we worship Him alone, but we have to stay alive for our family so we'll just do this for that reason," or "We will go along to get along, but we'll still worship God in our homes privately."

Thousands upon thousands all bowing down on that plain, and three guys remain standing. I don't care how awkward or out of place you've felt, you haven't experienced anything like that. Totally exposed, totally vulnerable, totally visible to the watching king. But not alone – they had each other.

Before long, the king hauled them to his presence and pressured them, and what unfolded was one of the most inspiring, moving, and instructive passages in all Scripture:

> "Furious with rage, Nebuchadnezzar summoned Shadrach, Meshach and Abednego. So these men were brought before the king, and Nebuchadnezzar said to them, 'Is it true, Shadrach, Meshach and Abednego, that you do not serve my gods or worship the image of gold I have set up?
>
> Now when you hear the sound of the horn, flute, zither, lyre, harp, pipe and all kinds of music, if you are ready to fall down and worship the image I made, very good. But if you do not worship it, you will be thrown immediately into a blazing furnace. Then what god will be able to rescue you from my hand?'
>
> Shadrach, Meshach and Abednego replied to him, 'King Nebuchadnezzar, we do not need to defend ourselves before you in this matter. If

we are thrown into the blazing furnace, the God
we serve is able to deliver us from it, and he will
deliver us from Your Majesty's hand.

But even if he does not, we want you to know,
Your Majesty, that we will not serve your gods
or worship the image of gold you have set up.'

Then Nebuchadnezzar was furious with
Shadrach, Meshach and Abednego, and his
attitude toward them changed. He ordered the
furnace heated seven times hotter than
usual and commanded some of the strongest
soldiers in his army to tie up Shadrach,
Meshach and Abednego and throw them into
the blazing furnace.

So these men, wearing their robes, trousers,
turbans and other clothes, were bound and
thrown into the blazing furnace. The king's
command was so urgent and the furnace so hot
that the flames of the fire killed the soldiers
who took up Shadrach, Meshach and
Abednego, and these three men, firmly tied, fell
into the blazing furnace.

Then King Nebuchadnezzar leaped to his feet in
amazement and asked his advisers, 'Weren't
there three men that we tied up and threw into
the fire?'

They replied, 'Certainly, Your Majesty.'

He said, 'Look! I see four men walking around in
the fire, unbound and unharmed, and the
fourth looks like a son of the gods.'

Nebuchadnezzar then approached the opening
of the blazing furnace and shouted, 'Shadrach,

STRANGERS

Meshach and Abednego, servants of the Most High God, come out! Come here!'

So Shadrach, Meshach and Abednego came out of the fire, and the satraps, prefects, governors and royal advisers crowded around them.

They saw that the fire had not harmed their bodies, nor was a hair of their heads singed; their robes were not scorched, and there was no smell of fire on them.

Then Nebuchadnezzar said, 'Praise be to the God of Shadrach, Meshach and Abednego, who has sent his angel and rescued his servants! They trusted in him and defied the king's command and were willing to give up their lives rather than serve or worship any god except their own God. Therefore I decree that the people of any nation or language who say anything against the God of Shadrach, Meshach and Abednego be cut into pieces and their houses be turned into piles of rubble, for no other god can save in this way.'"[82]

The most ardent unbeliever – a man so proud and arrogant he murdered, pillaged, looted, destroyed families, set up grand images and idols for the glorification of himself as god – comes to proclaim the unsurpassed majesty of the Biblical God.

No cultural foe we face, either political, academic, social, or intellectual, is as opposed to the Truth of God and His Word as was Nebuchadnezzar. How are they defeated and taught to obey?

Not by those willing to compromise and conform to the culture around them, but by those strangers who, strengthened by other believing friends, remain faithful to God in the face of any circumstance or threat.

Want to change the world? Be Daniel.

13
INTO THE DARKNESS

Okay, so it took me seven chapters, but I'm finally ready to tell you what my big concern is over the common Christian admonition to be "in the world, but not of the world."

My problem is our point of emphasis. We are so consumed with being "not of" this world, we pretend that was the focus of Jesus' prayer for His disciples. But it's not. Look again:

> "I am coming to you now, but I say these things while I am still in the world, so that they may have the full measure of my joy within them.
>
> I have given them your word and the world has hated them, for they are not of the world any more than I am of the world.

> My prayer is not that you take them out of the
> world but that you protect them from the evil
> one. They are not of the world, even as I am
> not of it. Sanctify them by the truth; your word
> is truth. As you sent me into the world, I have
> sent them into the world."[83]

For the first twelve chapters, we've outlined just what it means to be a "stranger, not of this world." But notice when Jesus was praying, though He stressed that principle multiple times, it was the "given," not the "action." Jesus assumes those that have crucified the flesh and have identified with Him are "not of this world." He *assumes* it. But what was the commission?

The action in this prayer is not on being "not of," but on being "sent into." That's why I titled this second section of the book, "Not of, but in;" because it puts the focus where Jesus put it – "in."[84]

Yes, we have died to self, put aside childish things, abandoned worldly pleasures. But that does not, and was never intended to equate to living lives of hermits, tucked away in sheltered, peaceful silence.

A couple years ago I started a backyard project for the ages. When we moved into our house, it came with an in-ground pool (a lifelong desire of mine). I want to get the most out of it, and have watched way too many do-it-yourself home improvement shows.

So I started dreaming – something the internet does not diminish. All it takes is a few clicks and you can quickly convince yourself how fast and easy it could be to complete some of the more elaborate undertakings.

Perusing some websites of backyard pools, I kept getting pulled in by the look of the larger commercial waterslides. Not the thin ones with a ladder that have a tiny slide and one small turn at the bottom. I mean the half-tube kind you find at a water park. I wanted one. No, I needed one.

But the one I settled on was far more expensive than we could reasonably afford, so I decided to budget for it. I'm still budgeting. But in order to be ready for when I hit the lottery that I don't play, I launched into some necessary groundwork.

The slide has to begin 8 feet off the ground. I coupled that requirement with my wife's long-expressed desire for an in-ground storm shelter (we live in the middle of tornado alley, and ever since watching *Twister* as a kid, she hasn't been a very big fan of no basement or shelter).

As it happened, Midwest Storm Shelters sold an underground cement shelter that stood from top to bottom, a little under 8 feet. I tore down our privacy fence and about 30 feet from the edge of our pool, I cleared a spot of land and had the underground storm shelter delivered and set on the top of the ground.

Then, I hauled in 200 tons of fill dirt, burying the shelter and rounding off the mound with a walkway and gentle slopes. We also shaped the front of it to do some landscaping beside the pool and a few other things. I've absolutely loved this project. But I'll tell you who didn't love it. My neighbors.

Apparently I became the talk of the neighborhood, with gawkers walking by regularly to try to comprehend what in the world had gotten into me.

The parents of a young woman I teach with live in our neighborhood and apparently called her over to come look at my construction project. "Just what is he doing back there?" they asked her. She wasn't sure but told them, "Well, he's pretty close to the Lord so maybe he knows something we don't." Perfect.

13 INTO THE DARKNESS

Evidently it's now the conventional wisdom around Davis Manor that I am constructing an apocalypse shelter where God will preserve my family and me during the unfolding Armageddon.

I've really thought about making the most of my neighborhood reputation and having some fun with it. You know, have my whole family get in our van with aluminum foil wrapped around our heads as we drive out of the neighborhood peering wearily into the sky above. Or even try to coordinate with the local zoo to have pairs of animals march in procession towards my backyard. It could be fun.

But anyway, a friend of mine commented recently that if the political environment continues on its present course, perhaps all our Christian families could retreat into my "doomsday shelter" and call it a life.

Obviously he was joking, but his comments do reflect the attitude of far too many disgruntled and discouraged believers these days. We express gratitude for our own salvation but then want to hunker down, spending our lives with bags packed, waiting on heaven to get here. What a waste.

We have been rescued from darkness and given the light of eternal truth not to guide our own personal steps as we sprint away from the dark world as fast as possible, but rather to guide our steps as we run *into* the darkness to rescue others.

That's what the Great Commission is about, after all.

> "Go and make disciples of all nations, baptizing them in the name of the Father and of the Son and of the Holy Spirit, and teaching them to obey everything I have commanded you."[85]

Notice the operative words there are "go," "make," "baptize," "teaching." Those are action words that make it imperative we do not retreat from the culture when we encounter resistance.

Jesus says "go" because we cannot fulfill His calling for our lives simply by patiently waiting for our own good living and love to attract the lost world to come to us.

Jesus says "make" and "baptize" because we cannot fulfill His calling for our lives by pretending that everyone else is okay just as they are – if they were, we wouldn't be told to "make" them into something different.

Jesus says "teaching" because we cannot fulfill His calling for our lives if we act like the way that seems right to the world doesn't end in death. It does. We know that and we must teach them to obey.

Frankly, I've never encountered anyone who enjoys being taught obedience – it's a discipline and requires submission of the will. Both of those are things contrary to human nature. Waiting to teach truth until the world embraces or enjoys being corrected and rebuked is a recipe for a wasted life.

Remember that the Holy Spirit tells us in 2 Corinthians 5:20 that we are "ambassadors" for Christ; we are the vessels through which God makes His appeal to a rebellious world. That is the term He uses: ambassadors.

You don't have to be a scholar of international or intergovernmental relations to know the one common trait of all ambassadors. They don't live at "home." Precisely the opposite, they leave and represent "home" in a foreign land. Bingo. That's us – or at least it's supposed to be.

If there's one thing I am quite certain of in our current era, it is that the American church is not doing a good job of being "ambassadors" for Christ in our world. In fact, Christians are unquestionably losing – in great strides, even – their ability to even penetrate a culture they once shaped and defined.

13 INTO THE DARKNESS

It is a fall from influence scarcely paralleled in the history of the world. Why did it happen?

Let's talk about that for a minute.

14
MISSIONARIES AREN'T
GREATER THAN MAYORS

In recent years I've been privileged to speak at several Christian youth conferences and conventions on a variety of topics. Sometimes when I am not the main speaker but instead presenting workshops or elective seminars at various times, I'll be able to sit in on other presentations. I always like to do that when I can in order to learn better communication styles, production approaches or new ideas that I can work into my own presentations to make them better.

Recently I sat through one that focused on "Finding Your Life Calling," which I thought was a really intriguing title given that the room was filled with all sorts of varied interests, abilities, strengths and opportunities. I wanted to see how the speaker managed to connect to each of those students in an engaging and specific way while taking on such a broad topic.

In fairness to him, it could be that the seminar was just poorly titled by the conference. But whatever the case, I felt really badly for what I assume are the vast majority of young people who attended that day but have no calling or desire to enter the paid pastoral ministry. The entire presentation was about becoming a minister, youth minister, worship leader, missionary, Christian disaster relief agency director, or head of a non-profit that specializes in carrying the Gospel along with necessary aid into impoverished, un-churched, or otherwise challenging areas.

Please don't misunderstand me; I believe that each of those are some great "life callings" for those whose life is called to them. How do you know if your life is called to them? I guess I've always been a little unclear on that myself.

It seems that we speak that way assuming that there will be this magical moment that occurs for every young person around the ages of 14-18 where God will appear and tell them like Abram to, "Go and settle in northern Indiana and begin repopulating the tri-state area."

I personally never had a moment like that, and so when young people ask me (as many do regularly) how they should know what to do with their lives, I always tell them what I did: personally identify your strengths, your passions and interests – in other words find what you love to do – and then use it to serve God.

That's how I would teach a "finding your life's calling" workshop. I'd stress that there are young people sitting in the seats in front of me who had more knowledge of what is happening under the hood of my jeep when they were 6 than I have today. I would tell them that they have always loved cars, understood them, worked on them and are incredibly good at grasping all things mechanical.

STRANGERS

And if that's the case, do that. Do that for as long as you have the passion to do it, and understand that God wants you to use it as a means to doing what we're all to be about: spreading the Gospel.

But how do you do that when you work under the hood? A million ways. How about the conduct and expectations you hold for yourself and all your employees? The way you talk, the way you work, the honesty of your business. The way you go above and beyond to serve your clients even at inconvenient times. The way you write off an expensive job that you know your customer (who has fallen on hard times) can't afford. You surprise them by attaching a note that says, "Paid in full...but only If you come sit with us at church this week." There is no limitation to how the Gospel of Christ can be shared and spread. We all have our own ministries regardless of our occupation.

I think we forget that sometimes, which is part of what has led to this unprecedented moment of Christians wielding so little influence in shaping the culture around us. We misunderstand our purpose here, and that has dire consequences.

Imagine the ambassador for the United States to a foreign country known for its genocide of Jews not objecting to that behavior because, "it's not our country, after all." Would that ambassador be effectively doing his job to promote the ideas, values and principles of the United States abroad?

Now that's actually a weak analogy because the sovereignty of God (for whom Christians are ambassadors) is far more all-encompassing than the global reach of the United States government. But it gives you an idea of the problem we have spawned.

Christians rightly understand that impacting a soul with the Gospel is the most important work to be done. While there is no questioning that reality, we irresponsibly jump from there to the absurd conclusion that in terms of importance to God's Kingdom, the missionary is greater than the mayor, the preacher greater than the prime minister, the priest greater than the president. This is nonsense.

No one questions that the humble missionary in India is impacting the eternal trajectory of souls when he converts a lost man to Christianity there. But had Churchill not defeated Hitler, the Third Reich would have certainly ruled India, if not the world. If that had occurred, would our humble missionary have been allowed to make his trip to the conquered German province? Very unlikely. Churchill too then impacts the eternal trajectory of souls by stopping the march of the evil tyrant.

Consider the great Christian statesman William Wilberforce of England who experienced a dramatic conversion to Christianity in 1786. His devotion to Christ nearly convinced him to leave Parliament and pursue a career as a clergyman. But in his personal diary, this man who single handedly would sway an entire nation's political leadership to bring about an end to the horrific slave trade, wrote these profound words that altered the course of human history:

> "My walk is a public one. My business is in the world, and I must mix in the assemblies of men or quit the post which Providence seems to have assigned me."[86]

After transforming Great Britain, Wilberforce wasn't content. Instead, he began taking this Christian political mission overseas and around the world. Countless Africans owed their freedom in no small part to Wilberforce's revelatory wisdom that a parliamentarian can be just as influential in doing God's work as a preacher.

As Hugh Hewitt correctly observes,

"If inviting non-believers to worship matters, then so does preserving the freedom to worship. If ministering to the needs of the poor is a mandate, then changing the policies creating poverty is very much within that mandate. And if building shelter in developing countries is part and parcel of a Christian's burden, then so is the destruction of the power of tyrants who oppress peoples around the globe."[87]

Far too many Christians have ignored this advice and have retreated to our Holy Huddles while our culture has declared outright rebellion to God. But here's the hard truth for the disengaged ambassadors amongst us:

Pretending there is no cultural war on God's authority doesn't make it go away. That war has been declared by the forces of this world as they seek to gain influence over an entire culture. When a war has been declared, you have only two options: engage or surrender. The truth is that in American society, Christians are largely not engaging. And why? What is the justification we offer for our surrender?

First, we say it doesn't matter. "Jesus didn't come to save a country, so we shouldn't waste our time on politics and those earthly pursuits of power," we self-righteously opine. It's certainly true that Jesus was no politician. His ministry was to impact the souls of man so powerfully that it would transform countries all over the world.

But to intimate that He and His message has no impact on politics or government is to be (1) blind to history, and (2) guilty of limiting the scope and power of the Messiah.

Imagine the stupidity of saying, "Well, Jesus wasn't a parent or a husband, so since He didn't find that important, I'm not going to worry about It either. There's more important things for the church to talk about than family." Or imagine if Wilberforce had said that about the African slave trade, "Jesus was no abolitionist of bodies, he was just worried about souls. So I'll just preach because any change has to begin with the heart."

This is exactly the statement being made by countless disengaged Christians throughout our culture, as the supreme authority of God is restricted and confined in its scope by its supposed ambassadors.

The truth is that God is either sovereign or He's not. If He is sovereign, then His truth and its transforming power is to go out into *all* the world. From dining rooms to boardrooms to schoolrooms to courtrooms, and yes, even to palaces and White Houses. And just who do you suppose are the ones entrusted and charged with taking it there?

Pretending that the fate of our civilization is of no eternal significance is stupidly shortsighted, and it foolishly collapses backwards into the "in, but not of" philosophy. Of course the collapse of the United States of America does nothing to end the Gospel of Jesus Christ. Of course the disciples faced far worse conditions than we would face even if the nation we live in ceased to exist tomorrow.

But just because the Gospel will survive doesn't mean that the collapse of our civilization wouldn't be a victory for Satan in his efforts to hamper the Great Commission.

Hewitt highlights that Sudanese Christians being tortured to death will not be helped by a shackled and empty American church.

Starving throngs in the third world will not be fed both physically and spiritually by non-existent missionaries, prevented to travel either by hostile economic or spiritual conditions here.

STRANGERS

Orphanages and widow's homes across the globe run by the compassion and financial investment of Christians will be strangled of support and shuttered should our civilization disappear.

Stop perpetuating the lie that God's truth applies only within the church walls or in a "religiously oriented" profession. It applies everywhere, all the time.

The second reason we retreat from our culture isn't born of ignorance like the first. Instead it's born of fear. We are scared of the conflict that we will encounter, either because of our reserved personality or because we make the assumption that conflict is automatically counterproductive to the message of Christ. It's funny how we come to that conclusion since Jesus didn't think so. In fact, Jesus told us to expect it if we are faithful to Him:

> "I am sending you out like sheep among wolves. Therefore be as shrewd as snakes and as innocent as doves."[88]

> "You will be hated by everyone because of me, but the one who stands firm to the end will be saved."[89]

> "If you belonged to the world, it would love you as its own. As it is, you do not belong to the world, but I have chosen you out of the world. That is why the world hates you."[90]

Why would Jesus do that to us? The answer is pretty simple and pretty motivating. He had an urgent message that needed to be proclaimed without reservation to the very ends of the earth. He needed it proclaimed from rooftops and mountaintops, pulpits and lecterns, doctors' offices, hospital rooms, nurseries, flower shops, dance halls, bars and brothels, abortion clinics, gay pride parades, Congressional hearings, town hall meetings, phone calls and at bedsides.

And He entrusted us with the privilege of being His messengers, no matter the place, no matter the time, no matter the cost. Truth is truth and we are called to speak it.

STRANGERS

Urgent and Unyielding

15
HELL

Allow me to issue a public service announcement at this point of the book. If by now you remain unconvinced that Christians are strangers, not of this world, but foreigners who have been sent into a hostile world for a specific purpose, please put this text down and find something better to do with your time. If my previous fourteen chapters were never able to achieve takeoff from your intellectual airfield, I don't hold out much hope that the final thirteen are going to help me avoid a crumpled mess at the end of your runway. Let's just both cut our losses and call it a day.

But for those of you who are with me on those realities, let me pause to ask a very significant question. Why? Why have we been sent intentionally into the world? Notice, I'm not asking "for what" have we been sent. I'm not asking about our purpose. I'd like to believe that we've already established our purpose is two-fold: (1) commissioned to make disciples (Matthew 28) and (2) sent to be ambassadors of Christ, God making His appeal through us (2 Corinthians 5:20).

I know "for what" we have been sent. My question is *why* did He send us? When I've asked that question from the stage or from behind a lectern, I have found that many believers know the answer, but they are afraid to say it. So let me say it.

Hell.

Hell is *why*. Eternal separation from God. Eternal darkness. Eternal fire. Eternal torment. That is what awaits every soul that has not been reconciled to God through Christ, and that is *why* we've been sent. The Father wants no one to perish, and so He sent His Son to prepare the only way out, and has sent us to share with everyone the escape plan. It's really that simple.

I'm always confused and somewhat annoyed by Christians who say things like, "Well, I don't want to scare people into heaven." What?! Why would you ever say something like that? Think of it from the perspective of earthly death as opposed to eternal death. How do you get your kids to not play in traffic? Do you tell them that the yard is so much more inviting, safe, soft and enjoyable? Do you tell them that Mommy and Daddy are so much more pleased with them when they stay away from the road? Or do you tell them that if they go out in the street they could be smashed by a car and die?

How do you get your kids to not drink the Drano under the kitchen sink? Do you tell them that their juice boxes and chocolate milk will taste so much better? Do you tell them that their little water bottles are easier to hold and drink from? Or do you tell them that if they drink that stuff it will eat their insides out in extraordinarily painful ways and kill them?

How do you get your kids to not wander into the swimming

STRANGERS

pool when you're not around? Do you tell them that it's so much more fun to swim with other people? Do you tell them that their lungs work a lot better on land than underwater? Or do you tell them that kids that swim alone can drown?

How do you get your older kids not to have pre-marital sex? Do you tell them that sex is so much better when you do it God's way? Do you tell them that the purpose of sex isn't selfish physical pleasure or that they will find fulfillment in ways they can't imagine if they just wait for their wedding night? Or do you show them gross pictures of what happens to their private parts if they engage in promiscuous sex?

See, we have no compunction or regret in "scaring" kids out of the street, out from under the kitchen sink, away from strangers, out of the pool or the pre-marital bedroom. Why? Because we love them and want them to be safe – we want to spare them from the awful fate of physical pain and death. Yet for some reason, we consider it unsophisticated, unrefined or disingenuous to "scare" people out of Hell.

I'm not surprised when God-denying fools try to use this line of argument to shame Christians from talking about Hell. Notorious God-denier Richard Dawkins spent time in his widely panned book *The God Delusion* suggesting that teaching children about Hell was a form of child abuse. While discussing the pedophilia scandal that rocked the Catholic church awhile back, Dawkins actually wrote these words:

> "[H]orrible as sexual abuse no doubt was, the damage was arguably less than the long-term psychological damage inflicted by bringing the child up Catholic [and therefore teaching him about hell] in the first place."[91]

To be fair to Dawkins (a courtesy he seemingly never offers believers, but I'm trying to model my chapter 11 advice, so please make a note of it), he wasn't directly comparing the two acts. He wasn't saying that sexual abuse is better to do to someone than talk to them about Hell. He was saying that the "long-term psychological effects" are more profound if you embed in them the "cold, immeasurable fear" of knowing people they love are going to Hell.[92] Still a ridiculously ignorant thing to say, but slightly less offensive I suppose.

When people like Dawkins who willfully suppress the truth say these kinds of things, it is unsurprising and somewhat banal. While I would agree it is emotionally abusing a child to convince them a *non-existent* horned, split-hooved, fire-breathing monster with a pitchfork was going to come and steal them away at night, I would think the precise opposite if such a monster really existed. The warning would go from hatefully manipulative to lovingly protective.

That's why I'm stunned when Christians are tempted to agree with arrogant God-deniers like Dawkins. Frankly I don't care what tactic I have to use to provoke someone into a committed relationship with Christ. Enticing them with the promise of heaven, scaring them with the threat of Hell, debating them into submission with the truth of the resurrection, reasoning with them to authenticate the Bible, loving them with the example of Christ-like grace – whatever it takes to get someone there works for me.

Which means the question we need to be asking ourselves is this: do we believe in Hell? Is it real? A real place? Is Satan real? A real being? The numbers might surprise you.

> 4/10 Christians (40%) strongly agreed that Satan "is not a living being but is a symbol of evil." An additional 2/10 Christians (19%) said they "agree somewhat" with that perspective.[93]

Just to make sure you caught that, almost 60% of American Christians (that is not talking about the general public, but specifically Christians) do not think that Satan is real. And in

STRANGERS

terms of Hell itself:

> "Only 32 percent of adults see hell as, 'an actual
> place of torment and suffering where people's
> souls go after death.'"[94]

Frighteningly, a large portion of the remaining 68% who don't believe in Hell are churchgoers. If you find that hard to believe, consider this exchange I recently had on my Facebook page with a woman who considers herself a Christian:

> *Woman: Well I am a Christian who does not
> believe in Hell. So I am on a journey to love
> others and to share Jesus but not because of
> the fear of Hell, but because life can be so
> much more today.*

> *Me: Every Christian I have known considers
> themselves a Christian because they believe
> Christ has "saved" them from the consequences
> of sin (Hell). What exactly did Jesus save you
> from if there is no eternal punishment for sin?*

> *Woman: He saved me from a hopeless life, he
> gave me grace, which I had been denied. I
> don't know if you have read or heard of Rob
> Bell who wrote the book Love Wins. If ever
> your (sic) curious how a Christian could not
> believe in Hell, there is a good explanation.
> Nothing about Hell relates to the God I know.*

It really is amazing how many people claim to follow Jesus yet consider Him to be a liar. After all, Jesus talked far more about Hell than He did about heaven. Sometimes I wonder if any of the sophisticates around Him accused Him of trying to "scare people" into heaven. But truthfully, as a follower of His, I'm content believing as Jesus did.

And that's why my standard answer to the question

whether or not I believe in Hell is this: "I believe in Hell as much as Jesus did." I much prefer to let the experts and elites argue with Jesus rather than with me. And here's what Christ and His Word tell us about Hell:

- It is an actual place originally designed by God for Satan and his demons.[95]

- No one is sent there unexpectedly; it is *chosen* by those who reject Christ.[96]

- It is a place of conscious torment.[97]

- It is eternal and irreversible.[98]

So let's make this as simple as possible: if you trust Jesus, there is no escaping the reality that Hell exists. And if it does exist, it is exactly why Jesus has sent you into the world. And if Jesus has sent you for that reason, that is exactly why there must be an urgency about us and our mission. It is simply impossible to conceive of any other focus or concern that should be more pressing or more motivating to a believer than the loving desire to spare any and every soul from such a ghastly and dreadful fate. This is precisely why the preacher Paul Washer exhorts,

> "If you do not talk much about sin, count on it, the Holy Spirit is not much in your ministry."[99]

If sin leads to a real place called Hell, then alerting and warning our fellow sinners of that impending doom apart from Christ should be our obsession. To the degree that it's not, it is more than fair to question either our belief in Hell's existence (and thus our trust in the Savior who warned of it) or the love we possess for our fellow man. And sadly that's exactly where the American church finds itself – failing its most pressing and urgent responsibility. Why? The next three chapters begin to answer that question.

16
MISLED CHRISTIANS

When I was in grad school several years ago I took a class required for my Masters called, "Moral Considerations and Political Violence." It was a summer course, and therefore mostly populated with students staring out the windows at the sun-drenched campus, undoubtedly longing to be anywhere but the place they found themselves. Personally, I was into the class. Perhaps that makes me sound like an insufferable nerd, but I have always been attracted to debate, particularly over moral and political philosophies.

It became almost inevitable those summer days that every class discussion would focus on the claims of exclusivity amongst the various faiths and belief systems that inform man's moral spectrum (the idea that one faith is right and the others are all wrong). My professor, a widely read and cultured younger guy, took great offense at any such notion of exclusivity. He often argued with me that, "There are literally millions of different paths and journeys a person takes spiritually and ethically – and that's just in our lifetime. When you consider the thousands of years before us and all those paths, the idea that just one set of moral ideas is the 'right set' becomes absurd."

Though I disagreed and did my best to explain why, there's no doubting the fact that his opinion is certainly the modern conventional wisdom. In a now widely-circulated clip from her old television program, the illustrious daytime host-turned-spiritual guru Oprah Winfrey popularized that wisdom:

> "One of the mistakes human beings make is believing that there is only one way to live and we don't accept that. There are diverse ways of being in the world. There are millions of ways to be a human being and many ways, many paths to what you call God. Her path might be something else and when she gets there she might call it the Light. But her loving and her kindness and her generosity, if it brings her to the same point it brings you, it doesn't matter whether she calls it God along the way or not. There can't possibly be just one way."[100]

Oprah must have been very popular amongst the Masters candidates in my class. As our debates wore on, other students would chime in from time to time, offering bits of human wisdom like the Hindu proverb that now annoyingly adorns inspirational nature pictures on many Instagram accounts:

> "There are hundreds of paths up the mountain, all leading to the same place, so it doesn't matter which path you take. The only person wasting time is the one who runs around the mountain, telling everyone that his or her path is wrong."

STRANGERS

Part of me hopes that the quote was something a drunk college hipster came up with late one night while his friends all said, "Duuuude, bro, that's deep. Better write that $#*& down, bro!" Surely the Hindus aren't so ignorant as to make this an actual proverb they claim for their faith. After all, notice the point of the statement is to argue for moral and ethical relativism; your path is right for you and I shouldn't tell you that you're wrong. But what is the "proverb" doing? It's telling someone that they're wrong when they tell others that they're wrong! This is circular stupidity masking itself as some kind of modern pseudo-intellectualism. Whenever I see this stuff posted, I want to comment and say, "Well quit running around the mountain telling me that I'm wrong to tell people they're wrong." But typically I don't.

I did, however, impress upon my professor that when Jesus told us there were two paths – one leading to the narrow gate of life and the other leading to the wide gate of destruction – He was making it pretty clear there weren't millions of ways, but just two to choose from. In fact, to highlight this point at speaking engagements, I sometimes take a large box of books. Each book represents a belief system upon which people build their lives and worldviews.

I take the Bible and put it in one stack. Then I take each successive book, whether it's Mohammed's *Quran*, Darwin's *Origin of Species*, Marx's *Communist Manifesto*, Smith's *Book of Mormon*, Sellers and Bragg's *Humanist Manifesto*, Vedavyasa's *Bhagavad-Gita* or the numerous others I have represented, and place them all in a second stack. When I've finished I tell the audience those are the two paths Jesus was talking about – we can trust the Word of God or we can trust the words of some man. Because in the end, apart from the Bible, that precisely what you have in any of those other texts.

It is surprisingly sad that so many Christians buy into the moral relativistic tripe that teaches "all paths are equally valid" given that it is a flagrant denial of Jesus' own words:

16 MISLED CHRISTIANS

> "Jesus answered, 'I am the way, the truth and
> the life. No one comes to the Father except by
> me.'"[101]

There's not much wiggle room for the universalist approach, I'm afraid. Jesus doesn't say He knows a way, He says *I am the way.* He doesn't say He speaks the truth, He says *I am the truth.* He doesn't say He is showing one way to live, He says *I am the life.* And He certainly doesn't indicate that He is but one of the many paths you can take to get to whatever it is that you call the "light." He is stating emphatically and without equivocation that *no one* will get to heaven except through relationship with Him.

Do we trust Jesus? Do we believe Him? If so, we won't be misled by the "many paths" lie, and instead recognize that saving others from Hell means bringing them to Jesus and Jesus alone. A true Christian urgently presses worldly people headed towards Hell that:

> "Salvation is found in no one else, for there is
> no other name under heaven given to mankind
> by which we must be saved."[102]

But though we have been cautioned not to fall prey to the "fine-sounding arguments of men,"[103] Christians are misled not only by the "many paths" lie but also the most misappropriated, abused and warped Scripture passage of all time: "Judge not, lest ye be judged."[104]

Any small foray into the social or political debates of our time will guarantee that you will be smacked over the head with the "Don't Judge Me" crowd. There are so many peculiarities and illogical contradictions that coincide with this line of argument it is actually shocking that so many Christians get tripped up by it.

First of all, often times the people using Matthew 7:1 to win an argument (i.e., "Oh yeah, well Jesus says not to judge! So why are you judging me?!") are the same people who (1) don't believe in Jesus, (2) hate the teachings of Jesus and refuse to abide by them, (3) are always arguing that Jesus has no place in political or social discussions (i.e., "Leave that in the church, not the public square!").

Secondly, the way these folks use the quote of Jesus is to equate "judging" with "declaring some action or idea wrong." Somehow they manage to miss the reality that they are using the quote to do what? To declare the action of disagreement wrong! By their own definition of the word "judging," they are guilty of the same offense.

So rather than fall for this fairly obvious perversion of Christ's words, those of us who actually care about them and take interest in His message should endeavor to understand what He actually taught in that famous Sermon on the Mount:

> "Do not judge, or you too will be judged. For in the same way you judge others, you will be judged, and with the measure you use, it will be measured to you.
>
> Why do you look at the speck of sawdust in your brother's eye and pay no attention to the plank in your own eye? How can you say to your brother, 'Let me take the speck out of your eye,' when all the time there is a plank in your own eye? You hypocrite, first take the plank out of your own eye, and then you will see clearly to remove the speck from your brother's eye."[105]

When reading the quote, "Do not judge" in its full context, it's not rocket science to figure out what Jesus is saying. He is warning against the haughty, self-righteous hypocrisy that finds fault only In others while ignoring the festering problems of self. That point becomes particularly clear when He brings up the sawdust and plank. How silly would a man look walking around with a giant board sticking from his eye when he approaches another person and says, "Here, let me check, I think you have something in your eye?" How silly you ask? As silly as the porn addict looks when he morally accuses the practicing homosexual of sexual immorality.

That's the point. Jesus is telling the porn addict to be careful not to go throwing around harsh and personal accusations of sexual immorality when he is guilty of the same. Why? Because the degree to which you condemn the sin is the degree to which God will condemn the sin in you. God's will is that you first find redemption and deliverance from your own sexual immorality so that you can effectively and credibly approach the homosexual offender and say, "Brother, I know better than most how awful sexual immorality can be and what it can do to your soul. Let me help you find the grace that I found to walk away."

Jesus is not counseling us not to care about the sawdust. If you've ever had a speck of sawdust in your eye, you know why He isn't – it's painful and potentially damaging if not removed. No, Jesus is not suggesting the sawdust be left alone. He is teaching that in order to effectively help the person plagued with it, we first need to make sure we aren't struggling with the same problem (in even greater degree).

Make sure you notice that Jesus encourages once the plank is removed from our own eye, we are then to go and help remove the speck. The "Don't Judge Me" crowd does not understand the distinction; nor do they care to grasp the perfect moral lesson of Jesus. They would regard any effort, made at any time, by anyone, to remove the speck as "unloving judgment."

But for a Christian, the instruction is clear: if you love, you judge…but you do it with a clean conscience before God (a "plankless" eye). If that statement seems radical to you, it's because you've been listening to the world on this issue for too long. Listen instead to the voice of Scripture that tells us:

"He who is spiritual judges all things."[106]

Of course we do! How can mature Christians obey Scripture's wisdom to avoid those with bad character, those with violent tendencies, those who are fools, those who dishonor God, those who are insolent, those who will cause us to stumble, if we are not "judging" or discerning right from wrong, and good from bad? Speaking of mature Christians, the book of Hebrews says they,

"Have power of discernment that are trained to distinguish good from evil."[107]

That discernment allows us to, as Jesus put it just moments later in His Sermon on the Mount, "know them by their fruits."[108]

Earlier I said that it was shocking that so many Christians fell for the world's abusive mistreatment of Jesus' statement to not judge. The term shocking is greatly underestimating the seriousness of our failure to pierce through this Scriptural abuse that threatens our entire faith.

After all, if a Christian begins accepting the notion that the power of discernment is bad, of that being trained to distinguish good from evil is inappropriate, we will have upended the entire purpose of Christ sending us into the world.

How can we fulfill the Great Commission by "teaching them to obey" if we do not judge whether or not they are yet disciples? How can we fulfill our command to represent God's truth as His ambassadors to the world if we do not discern the difference between the wide and narrow path? How can we fulfill our privilege to lead others to a saving relationship with Christ if we refuse to distinguish for them the difference between light and dark?

131

Theologian Dr. Michael Brown counsels,

> "Should we not judge human trafficking as evil,
> or abortion as evil or ISIS as evil? In the days of
> slavery and segregation here in America, should
> Christians not have judged these wicked
> practices as evil? …
>
> By all means, we must obey the Lord's call to
> make righteous judgments. As Jesus said in
> John 7:24, 'Do not judge according to
> appearance, but practice righteous
> judgment.'"[109]

That's the message of Christ: don't judge hypocritically, but judge righteously. Without doing so, we are uselessly ineffective in the campaign we've been sent into the world to conduct, and Satan's grip on that world grows tighter. God forbid it.

17
COMPROMISING
CHRISTIANS

Besides being misled by the fine-sounding arguments of men, there's a second reason many Christians today are failing their urgent responsibility to warn others about the Hell that awaits sinners outside of Christ. We compromise for the sake of "getting along."

Obviously we are to "make every effort to live in peace with everyone,"[110] but too often for the sake of convenience and comfort, we equate peace with capitulation, goodwill with retreat. Simply look at how the church is handling the current manifestation of the sexual revolution in America. Scriptural teaching on human sexuality is as clear and well-defined as any other topic you can find. Yet, despite feeling no need to pacify or placate the "Theft Community" or the "Swindler Community" or the "Adulterous Community" or the "Lying Community," so many Christians fall all over themselves to coddle and indulge the sinful urges of those in the so-called "LGBT Community." It's bizarre.

If I have spent more time addressing the sin of same-sex attraction in this book than any other, it is only because it is, without question, the one cultural sin where Satan's manipulations, calculations and wiles have Christians completely confounded. Here's what I mean by that.

Not one Christian I know struggles to tell an adulterer they are sinning and need to repent. Not one church I've encountered struggles to tell a liar they are sinning and need to repent. Not one denomination I'm aware of struggles to tell a thief they are sinning and need to repent. But the number of Christians who struggle, churches who stumble, and denominations who surrender when it comes to telling a person caught up in homosexuality, bisexuality, or transgenderism that they are sinning and need to repent is simply astounding.

Satan has convinced so many wearing the name of Jesus that people who practice homosexuality are too delicate and fragile to be told the truth. And we stupidly listen to our enemy. We give quarter to Satan's deception somehow managing to convince ourselves that it is the Christ-like thing to do. We puff our chests out and prattle on about "opening a dialogue with the LGBT community." People practicing lesbianism, homosexuality, bisexuality and transgender behavior do not need a dialogue from us – they need to be lovingly told the truth that they will not hear from anywhere else.

Satan is intent on destroying those poor people by locking them into their sinful urges and convincing them through society's megaphone that their sin is their "identity." All that stands in the way of his success is the church's voice of truth –

STRANGERS

the same voice of truth we are willing to use to address all other sinners and sins. Do we love those practicing homosexuality less that we would withhold from them the promise of redemption that we have found ourselves and offered to everyone else?

Sadly, the answer I see repeated time and again is yes.

Several years ago when I was in college, you could be pretty well guaranteed that on any given day if you cycled through our multi-disc CD changer you would find an album or two of the Christian band "Jars of Clay." They were big then, and for the most part I really enjoyed their music.

If you would have told me during that era of my life that in just a few short years I would be having a public argument with the lead singer of that band, Dan Haseltine, I wouldn't have believed it. First, I wouldn't have believed that someone as popular as Haseltine would ever have reason to know my name. Second, I wouldn't have believed what it was that we would be arguing over: the authority and reliability of God's Word as it relates to sexual morality. After all, we are both Christians. How could we possibly find disagreement over Scriptural supremacy?

But that's exactly what happened. Looking through my Twitter feed one day, I came across some bizarre tweets from Haseltine that grabbed my attention. He started off this way:

> "Not meaning to stir things up, BUT...Is there a non-speculative or non 'slippery slope' reason why gays shouldn't marry? I don't hear one."

First of all, when someone leads off with those six words, it is clear they are intending to do one thing: stir things up. And that's precisely what he did. When the lead singer of a well-known Christian band wades into a major cultural and political issue, coming down on the side opposed to orthodox

Christianity, it's going to make waves. Several folks responded to Haseltine and pointed out the obvious: a Christian makes Scripture his final authority for all moral judgments. Therefore, given that Scripture condemns homosexual relationships and Jesus affirms the man/woman design for marriage and family, that should be reason enough for Dan.

I would have left it alone, but Haseltine didn't take the rebuke well at all. Instead he fired this back:

> "I don't particularly care about Scripture's
> stance on what is 'wrong.' I care more about
> how it says we should treat people."

If the fact that a prominent Christian actually typed and published the words, "I don't particularly care about Scripture's stance on what is wrong" isn't a clear sign of how effectively Satan has made incredible headway against the church in this battle over the souls of the same-sex attracted, I don't know what would be. That statement is simply a dazing call for retreat from the eternal battlefield. And logically, it's a complete mess, which should really come as no surprise. When you abandon the Word of God as your moral guidepost, you end up embarrassing yourself in a maze of ethical contradictions.

Haseltine managed to do it in just two sentences. In his first sentence he declares that he doesn't care what Scripture says is wrong. But in his very next sentence he declares that he does care what Scripture says about how to treat people. Ummm, why is that, Dan? Because there is a way to treat people that Scripture says is…wait for it…wrong?! I thought we were unconcerned with right and wrong? This is what happens when you attempt to calibrate your moral compass by worldly standards instead of staying tethered to the immovable Word of God; you begin journeying in a direction that logic just doesn't follow. And that's right where Dan found himself with the next tweet he sent out:

STRANGERS

"Because most people read and interpret
scripture wrong. I don't think scripture 'clearly'
states much of anything regarding morality."

Someone close to him, some brother in Christ, the bass
guitarist for the band, anybody within a 10 mile radius, needed
to go and pull Dan's hands from the keyboard and ask him to
slowly back away before he damaged his credibility or (more
importantly) the cause of Christ any more than he had already
done. That is simply an irresponsible and inexcusable
statement. If Scripture isn't the purest, most reliable guide for
morality on earth, what is? It is an error of colossal proportions
to write something like that when you have such a public
platform.

So at this point, I decided to attempt to bring about some
form of clarity to the gigantic moral quagmire that had been
birthed. Understanding that Twitter, with its 140 character
limit, is not the best place to dig into matters of spiritual
importance, I offered this:

"In the interest of open dialogue, I'd like to
invite Dan on my program next week to discuss
this issue. Interest?"

Dan replied:

"I'm not interested in drumming up controversy
to help increase your audience. That's what this
is, right?"

To be sure, Dan had already drummed up controversy with
his ignorant statements about the Bible's unreliability and lack
of moral clarity. My offer was to help tamp down the
controversy by reaffirming what I thought we both agreed upon
– the inerrancy of Scripture. So I responded:

"Dan, many caught up in sin are reacting to
your words encouraged to persevere in their

sin. That's my concern, not audience."

Dan replied:

> "Which sin? Selfishness? Greed? Lying?
> Stealing? Lusting? I don't think a radio show
> will change that. But by the grace of God..."

Well of course it is only the grace of God by which we are delivered from our sins. The problem is that Dan left open the idea that one of those sins did not require deliverance. Which is what I wrote back to him:

> "That's the point. You condemn all those you
> list but not homosexuality? Why? Why deny
> homosexuality the full counsel of God?"

Dan never responded to me again. Sad, really. But not because a Christian I had previously held in high esteem proved himself to be fallible or fallen. Not because I would always remember having to battle him over the moral superiority of God's Word above all things every time a Jars of Clay song comes on the radio. But because of the tragically misleading message Dan had sent to this one select group of sinners.

After the Twitter exchange, I reached out to a friend of mine who is ex-gay. He lived the lifestyle for years before coming to Christ and, as he puts it, realizing he could find his identity in Jesus rather than his sinful attractions. For those who say God doesn't still perform miracles, I look at this man justified and sanctified by the blood of Jesus, see a life turned completely around and say you're crazy.

I was curious to know whether he thought in my conversation with Haseltine I misrepresent myself. Was I too harsh? Was I missing something? These were my questions, and this was the response:

Pete, I've seen these kinds of conversations

STRANGERS

before. I watched them intently when I was in the lifestyle. When you're caught up in sin, you look for anything to justify it. That 'still small voice' constantly tells you what you're doing isn't right. But when you can find anything, anyone, to say it's okay, you cling to it. We find ways to justify our sins, not just homosexuality.

And right now one of the reasons it is so hard for people to break free from the sin of homosexuality is because of all the approval and embrace of it in our culture.

I had never thought of this before, to be honest. I knew, like other sins, the longer a person persisted in it, the harder it became to break free. I knew, like other sexual sins, that the intimate nature of relationships can add layers of emotional attachment on top of the mere physical enjoyment of the sin, increasing the difficulty to escape. But it's true that no other sin enjoys as much affirmation, embrace and normalization in our culture as does homosexuality. Even something as common as divorce still bears a negative stigma – it's something you feel bad for doing. Homosexuality is a celebrated sin. The response continued:

Let there be no mistake, you are speaking truth and Dan Haseltine is at best confused, at worst a willing participant in the deception of sinners. But that is not the way this will be perceived by those who are caught up in homosexuality. You look like the judgmental and unloving one. Dan looks like the open-minded, loving one.

When I was a practicing homosexual, I would have clung to his public 'questions' and refusal to say that homosexuality was a sin. I would have said to myself, 'See, here's the lead singer of a Christian band who knows this is 'who I am' and that it can't be wrong in God's eyes.' I would have let the lie sink deeper in me that those who were telling me it is wrong are the ones with the problem – not me. And if you look at the comments that others made throughout your conversation with him, you can see that is exactly what is happening.

It's heartbreaking from my perspective because I can put myself in their shoes and I just want to cry for them being so lost and mired in their sin. Dan Haseltine may not know it, but every moment that goes by, his refusal to speak the plain words of Scripture is attaching another set of chains that truth will have to bust through if that soul is ever to be saved. His silence and public questioning of Truth have undoubtedly put up huge stumbling blocks for many. It's tragic beyond words.

Wow. Look at that second to last sentence. Is that you? Is that us? Are we silent about this one sin? Or worse, are we publicly questioning whether or not the behavior is sin? If so, far from being loving agents administering God's compassion to a hurting world, we are Satan's tools, weaving deception from within the ranks of His ambassadors. We are setting up stumbling blocks rather than knocking down strongholds. And there are many within Christendom who are far worse offenders of this betrayal than Dan Haseltine.

For instance there was Rob Bell, the infamous megachurch minister whose 2011 book *Love Wins* (the one referenced in my Facebook exchange last chapter) questioned the existence of Hell, and thus the tenets of orthodox Christianity. Unsurprisingly, the journey from questioning Biblical authority to rejecting the doctrines of Christ was a short one, and Bell left his ministerial role on a search for what he called, "a more forgiving faith...one that can keep pace with the rising 'waterline of culture.'"[111]

Then there are those who don't want to abandon the Christian faith as Bell did, but instead rewrite it (or "reinterpret it") to keep up with that "waterline" Rob mentioned. Take Tony Campolo, who over time has fallen into the dangerous trap of letting his politics inform his faith rather than the other way around. To help facilitate Christian embrace of far left political causes, Campolo has been complicit in helping start the heretical "Red Letter Christian" movement that suggests the words of Jesus are more divinely inspired than the rest of Scripture. Heresy.

But long before Campolo became Bill Clinton's spiritual adviser and thus a mouthpiece for liberal causes wrapped in Christian clothing, I remember hearing a powerful piece of preaching from him. I have searched for the text or even audio of the message without luck, but the words have been seared into my memory.

In the midst of an intense plea for believers to seek and save the lost, Campolo thundered through my radio, "At this very moment there are thousands of people dying and going to Hell and many of you don't give a 'darn'." You probably figured out from the quotes that he didn't say darn. I could have heard the gasp from the audience when he uttered that word if it weren't for the fact that I gasped too. What kind of preacher uses profanity in the pulpit? Then Campolo, in hushed tones, dropped this line: "Proof of that fact is the reality that many of you are more consumed and focused on the word I just said than the shocking truth that thousands are now in Hell." Like I said, it was a powerful piece of preaching.

So how disappointing for me now to see that Campolo is affirming the sin of homosexuality and the affront to God's design for family by encouraging same-sex "marriage." How is it that a man who so powerfully impacted me with the unequaled and unparalleled responsibility of believers to urgently reach condemned sinners with saving Truth now calls for the church to silence that Truth so as not to appear "disapproving" of the sin of homosexuality?[112] There's that focus on the "cultural waterline" again.

Christian blogger and columnist Rachel Held Evans has her eyes firmly fixed on the ebbs and flows of culture as well. Using her widely read blog site as her platform, Evans repeatedly chastises the church for its refusal to abandon orthodox Christian teaching on sexual morality and even Biblical inerrancy, suggesting that clinging to such principles makes Christianity too judgmental and yes, culturally irrelevant.

In a *Washington Post* op-ed she gave lip service to the idea that Christianity shouldn't be about a hip veneer or a better style and image. But even if she eschews aesthetic relevance, she demands doctrinal relevance. She wants the church's teachings to reflect cultural norms and fads, thereby shedding its reputation of being too "judgmental" and "exclusive."[113] In other words, she yearns for a church more open-minded and inclusive of alternative ideas, beliefs and lifestyles.

I suppose there is some merit to what she is saying if the sole purpose of the church is to fill seats on Sunday mornings. If the mission of the church is nothing more than a relentless ambition to "affirm" everyone from all walks of life, then her counsel is spot on.

After all, speaking the exclusivity of Christ – that whole "no man comes to the Father except by me" thing – or preaching repentance is not going to make anyone feel affirmed. Everyone can see how painfully un-hip such a message is in contemporary American society.

In fact, churches committed to that outdated way of thinking might be accused of acting like some prudish carpenter of antiquity whose obsessive devotion to unpopular notions of right and wrong, good and evil, consigned him to the outskirts

STRANGERS

of society rather than the mainstream, to preaching from hillsides rather than from behind gold-crusted lecterns.

It's curious, isn't it? Somehow American Christians convinced themselves that becoming more like Jesus of Nazareth would make them more attractive to the world; but the exact opposite is true. After all, why would they treat us any different than they treated Him? Confusing that reality has the American church all kinds of backwards. If the world adores us for the words we speak, it is not because those words are loving and good. It is because they are cowardly and compromising. And that's the real problem we face in our churches.

I readily admit I don't boast the credentials of so many weighing in on the unfolding collapse of American Christianity. But I humbly submit that if the church wants to stop the bleeding, it should stop worrying about the praise of men and instead seek the applause of heaven. How is that done?

At a recent 414 Retreat I run for Christian high school seniors about to head to college, I asked them to name 5 figures from Scripture that God used in a powerful way. Their list included Noah, Moses, Elijah, John the Baptist and Jesus. Question for the American church: how relevant to their respective cultures were those guys?

Noah was a laughingstock, Moses was exiled and hated, Elijah had a bounty on his head, John the Baptist lost his head, and Jesus lost a popularity contest with a despised murderer named Barabbas – all because they were each committed to speaking a truth that no one in their time wanted to hear.

True Christianity is confrontational. It is an open and courageous rebellion being conducted deep within enemy-occupied territory. It is counter-cultural, not culturally relevant. It alone recognizes that there is no love without truth.

If Christ's church dies in the United States, it's only because

143

it committed suicide on the altar of relevance.

18
SCARED CHRISTIANS

For those believers who are neither misled nor compromising, there remains one final, unfortunate reality as to why we are failing to urgently speak the truth to a dying world: we're scared.

The fear can take on various forms, but ultimately it comes down to us not wanting the discomfort, unease, or potential conflict that arises when you tell someone what they're doing isn't good or right. A friend of mine in the world of media sent me a text message not long ago to encourage me in the raging battle over religious freedom in America. He knew that I was being called the standard litany of names assigned to people of conscience these days: bigot, hater, discriminator, etc.

In his message he said, "It's amazing and sad how many Christians are scared to say it like it is. I'm inspired by you." It was very kind of him to take the time to send me that message, and I replied by asking if he was taking some heat for his beliefs also, given his position. His reply, while honest, was pretty funny: "Not to this point, but I'm a lot bigger coward than you." First of all, I don't think that's true. But secondly, how tacky of me to turn a text of encouragement into a self-flagellation over personal cowardice. Oops.

But since he came up with the term, many times "cowardly Christians" will tell me that they are just trying to live an inoffensive life as we Christians are supposed to do. I don't buy it for a second. I guarantee that if you give me 24 hours of observing you, watching your interactions with coworkers, viewing what you post online, reading your text messages, that we will discover together you are not making great strides to live "inoffensively."

That's not a criticism, but rather a humble observation of your human nature. For the most part, the same people who don't want to offend someone with God's views on sin have no problem whatsoever offending people when it comes to their favorite sports teams, the local annexation issue, or the presidential campaign. They lack the courage to warn someone away from Hell, but they aren't about to let somebody think Andrew Luck is a better quarterback than Aaron Rodgers. They lack the guts to confront someone about a sin that will wreck their lives, but if you try to annex their house into the city, there's going to be a fight.

We have the courage and willingness to offend others on far less significant issues than the fate of their soul. That tells me what we are lacking when it comes to our urgent purpose as Christians isn't courage, but will.

Still others protest that it's just not in their personality to speak truth. I heard this often from folks when I hosted my radio show. It would go something like this: "Peter, you do a radio program where you talk to people about this stuff regularly and are used to confrontation. I just wasn't wired that way at all." First of all, I completely agree that God gives each of us different strengths. He gifts us with different personality traits and blesses our character with a wide range of temperaments. That's true not just in our time, of course, but throughout Scripture.

Go back and look at that list of Biblical faith heroes I offered up in the last chapter. Except let's trade Esther in for Jesus – it gives us a woman for one thing. And putting Christ in the list might be viewed as cheating given His perfection and our...well, stunning imperfections. Now evaluate what we know of each of their personalities:

> Noah was a humble man who lived quietly and peacefully in his time.

> Moses was one conflicted dude. He had been like a prince in Egypt, raised in the palace. Yet he was haunted by his own ethnic origins and eventually snapped, committing murder. He fled to become a shepherd before reluctantly dragging himself back to Egypt where he had to enter the courts of Pharaoh himself.

> Elijah was the very definition of a hothead. Unstable, perhaps. In one moment he wants to charge King Ahab and blow up the building, then he becomes suicidal, then he's ready to call down fire amidst an epic performance of godly sarcasm on Mt. Carmel.

> Queen Esther was a reserved woman who didn't want the throne, was given the throne, didn't want to make a scene, but made a scene to save her people.

> John the Baptist was a rebel in every sense of the word. He didn't care what people thought

of him or said of him. He was a voice crying in
the wilderness eating locust, growing long hair,
and loving every minute of it.

So there you go – about every personality trait you can
imagine in those five characters. But despite their different
personalities and character descriptions, do you notice one
thing in common? God called on *all* of them to speak truth:

- For Noah it was on the steps of the Ark.

- For Moses it was in the presence of "god on earth."

- For Elijah it was a confrontation with hundreds of
  Baal's evil prophets.

- For Esther it was in the spotlight of the King's
  chambers.

- For John the Baptist it was in the wilderness to
  anyone passing by.

No matter your personality, no matter your place, your
calling is the same. Speak truth urgently as if souls depended
on it. Because they do.

Be on guard also for an insidious lie that Satan tells loudly
and often. It's the lie that equates telling hard truths with being
un-loving. Not long ago a friend of mine, Amanda McKinney,
wrote an excellent blog post about what real Christian love is.
It stuck with me because both Amanda and I are at the same
point in our lives – raising children.

She points out that when you're the parent of young
children you are likely to hear (quite regularly) your kids scream
at you how you're a terrible parent and must hate them or
something. I caught my oldest daughter Addie doing this on my
cell phone camera once, and I use it in various speaking
presentations to illustrate the point. Addie was misbehaving,

breaking a rule that she knew not to break. My wife got on her about it and Addie crosses her arms, starts to pout and says in the most offended voice she can muster, "I guess you don't love me anymore." My wife, always the delicate one, responds with, "Addie, that's just dumb." But it wasn't dumb to Addie. Since Jenny was telling her she couldn't do something, there was really only one conclusion her 6-year-old mind could come to: "Mommy doesn't love me." After all, if Mommy did love her, she would obviously let her do *whatever* she wanted to do, right? The pinnacle of love is complete and utter permissiveness, is it not?

Amanda points out in her blog that if parents actually started believing their kids when they said that, if they started "loving" children the way the kids *wanted* to be loved rather than needed to be loved, there would truthfully be no loving parents anymore. Why? Because it's patently obvious that love isn't always affirming, it isn't always condoning, it isn't always saying "yes."

Christians, we could do well to learn that lesson. The moment someone who isn't a Christian says they don't feel loved – or worse, they say they feel "judged – we immediately begin believing that we did something wrong. Or even if *we* don't, we are soon buried beneath an avalanche of criticism from our Christian brethren rebuking us for "driving someone from the faith;" we are pummeled until we sheepishly issue some kind of apology for not showing the "love of Christ."

Go back to that scene on my cell phone camera for a minute. What would have happened if instead of filming and chuckling to myself, I jumped up and took Addie's side? What if the moment she proclaimed that Mommy doesn't "love her anymore," I flipped out on Jenny and said, "What have you done?!"

What if I bombarded Jenny in front of Addie and our other two kids, with reproach and scolding, belittling her and telling her how much she was damaging our relationship with our children. What message would that send to Jenny? Or worse, what kind of confused message would that send to our kids?

Welcome to the modern American church where believers can't wait to tag the "judgmental Christians" as they proudly assume the mantle of "loving Christian." It's what Amanda calls, "Good Cop/Bad Cop Christianity." She writes,

> "For awhile, the Church tried to pull off a Good Cop/Bad Cop routine when someone sinned within the congregation – with people like me playing the bad cop, and the non-confrontational folks just waiting quietly for the uncomfortable stuff to be handled so they could go back to planning showers and pitch-ins.

> But now, we're to the point where the "good cop" Christians don't want the "bad cops" to have a role at all.

> In fact, now the former good-cops are sharing articles about why the police force should stop "policing" altogether. [i.e., "Don't judge" Facebook posts]

> ...and the nonbelievers keep shrieking, 'Why can't you other Christians be more like these nice ones???' It's exactly what happens when the 'fun' parent throws the rule-enforcer under the bus.

> Thanks for worrying about my reputation, "Good, Loving" Christians...But you and I are supposed to be on a team. You're causing the anarchy...because you'd rather do away with tough love and avoid rocking the boat. You're

worried about upsetting children, so you're letting them take over."[114]

I really can't imagine a more important parallel for all believers to read right now than the one McKinney just made. Just like children who don't know any better, the lost among us feel "judged" and "unloved." But if we Christians truly believe we do know better than them (we do believe that, right?), then why are we concerning ourselves with their opinion of us anymore than we fret over our kids declaring we don't love them anymore? If the godless sinners among us have no moral compass, why are we listening to them to determine if we're heading in the right direction?[115]

I can hear the pushback from a mile away, and it sounds like this: "But Peter, but Peter, Scripture tells us that 'they will know we are Christians by our love!' If they don't feel loved then they won't know we're Christians!" This is why I sometimes loathe modern praise songs (although I think we're stretching it a bit to call this one "modern"). Those are the lyrics of the song, popularized by (who else) Jars of Clay, after all:

"And they'll know we are Christians by our love,
by our love
Yes, they'll know we are Christians by our
love."[116]

With all due respect to the Jars of Clay guys, forget the song and listen to what the Savior actually said:

"By this everyone will know that you are my disciples, if you love one another."[117]

The world will know we are Christians by the love that we show to one another. Putting it bluntly to all the "Good-cop Christians" who are so eager to earn admiration from the world for their "love," it isn't Jesus' idea of loving to throw your brothers and sisters in Christ under the bus publicly for their allegiance to the Truth. We're on the same team.

S╋RANGERS

19
WHAT IS "LOVING" LIKE JESUS?

My wife and I recently took an anniversary trip to Walt Disney World where we had honeymooned ten years before. While relaxing in the resort pool one afternoon we both noticed him walking across the deck about the same time. With no pre-planning or communication, we both looked at each other and exclaimed simultaneously, "Jesus!"

No worries if you're reading this, you didn't miss the rapture. The Middle Eastern looking man with a scruffy beard and wavy hair was heading over to get a frozen alcoholic beverage for he and his wife. Yes, I know Jesus turned water into wine, but He didn't have a wife, so I'm fairly confident this wasn't the second coming. But as I watched him, it dawned on me that If our kids had been there to hear Jenny and I say that, they wouldn't have understood. Because every image of Jesus they have seen in their children's Bibles, our family picture Bible, the cartoon Bible clips we watch every so often, and even the Christmas nativity scenes, depict Jesus as Caucasian.

Some people get really worked up about that, even people you wouldn't expect. Peruse atheist websites some time and you are likely to see someone mocking the ethnic representation of "whitey Jesus" at the Creation Museum or Western art museums. To be honest, I don't really care about that. I'm far more concerned with the misrepresentation of who Jesus was than what He looked like. I find the former far more irresponsible than the latter.

Because whereas artist renderings will ultimately be based on conjecture, the testimony of Jesus' life, words and instruction is inspired and accurate. Yet I can't count the number of times I've heard a believer, unwilling to engage their Christ-given mission to urgently seek and save the lost from their sins, tell me, "I just want to model Jesus in the way I live."

Listen, if you avoid confrontation in order to model Jesus, you don't know Jesus. Remember His words that I mentioned earlier:

"Do you think I came to bring peace on earth?
No I tell you, but division."[118]

Simply put, Jesus was the most controversial figure in human history. If you struggle to believe that, ask yourself why it is that 2,000 years after he left the surface of the earth, the mere mention of his name by a 17-year-old at a graduation ceremony can instigate lawsuits and atheist organizations losing all control of their bodily functions? If you don't think He was a controversial figure, ask yourself the even simpler question of why He was crucified.

If you say you want to follow and model Jesus, this would

be a helpful thing to know, would it not? Jesus wasn't put to death for His compassion and love. He wasn't pierced with nails and a spear because He was healing people or preaching morality. He wasn't hung on a cross with thorns slicing his brow because He fed the hungry or talked to Samaritans.

So why was He tortured to death? Even the Roman governor Pilate couldn't find fault in Him. Yet the masses demanded the release of a murderous thug named Barabbas just so they could be rid of Jesus. The authorities knew He had done no wrong, to the point that when ordering His execution, Pilate publicly washed his hands of responsibility. But because Jesus was so unbelievably controversial, they ordered this innocent man to be executed in the most humiliating of ways just to unload Him.

Why?

There is one answer: Jesus was killed because He was speaking Truth that the "power" of that day found offensive. Jesus engaged His culture with Truth they didn't want to hear – so they killed Him.

If you want to "live as Jesus," that's what you do too. Because remember, Jesus not only lived it, but he applauded others who did so. To society's elites and scholars, John the Baptist was one of the most reviled men you could imagine. He was an unkempt, unwashed, unsophisticated lunatic preaching madness in the wilderness. He dared to call out the culture for its sin, ripped the pious abusers of religion for their hypocrisy, and demanded that all men come into obedience with the One who was to come. Not exactly a culturally comfortable ministry.

And what did the Son of God say of John the Baptist?

> "Truly I tell you, among those born of woman there has not risen anyone greater than John the Baptist."[119]

19 WHAT IS "LOVING" LIKE JESUS?

What kind of applause do you seek? The fading lights of worldly stardom, or the praise of God's Son? If you truly seek the latter, you do as John the Baptist. You do as Jesus instructed you:

> "Teaching them to obey everything I have commanded you."[120]

> "There's a way that seems right unto a man, but the end thereof is death."[121]

Remember, if men in our culture are merely acting according to the way that seems right to them, they will never change unless they are confronted with the reality that their way isn't right. When confronted, not all of them will like it. Not all of them will react as we want. Not all of them will heed our warning. But some will. And if we trust the Word of God is true, if we know that the path they are currently walking leads them to death, why would we not confront and save whomever we can?

If you want to be a Christ follower, you do as Christ. For those who say, "But doesn't that mean acts of service, compassion, feeding and clothing? Doesn't it mean acts of love?" Of course it does. But notice how Jesus conducted so many of His "acts of compassion."

In John 4 when He meets the woman at the well, Jesus doesn't carefully dance around her sin. He confronts it head on, telling her that He knows the man she is living with is not her husband. His act of compassion was speaking to her truthfully, and she went away amazed saying, "This man told me everything I ever did." His miracle was to bring about a changed heart.

In Luke 7 when He forgives the sinful woman at the Pharisee's home, Jesus again praises the woman for her faith that He alone can save her from her "many sins." His act of love was speaking to her truthfully about her need for redemption, and she went away forgiven.

In Luke 5 when the paralytic is lowered in front of Jesus on his mat, what is the first thing that Jesus says? He tells the man his sins had been forgiven. And it was at that point that the teachers of the law and the Pharisees all went crazy, infuriated at the arrogance of a lowly carpenter's son who would suggest He had the authority to forgive sins. So (please catch this) to prove He had the authority to do just that (something far more significant and important), Jesus told the man to pick up his mat and go:

> "Jesus knew their thoughts and said to them, 'Why do you think such things? Is it easier to say, 'Your sins are forgiven,' or to say, 'Get up and walk'? I will prove to you, then, that the Son of Man has authority on earth to forgive sins.' So he said to the paralyzed man, 'I tell you, get up, pick up your bed, and go home!'

> At once the man got up in front of them all, took the bed he had been lying on, and went home, praising God."[122]

In other words, the entire purpose of the physical healing was to demonstrate He had the authority to do something He viewed as far more significant: forgive a man's sins. When Jesus reminds those listening that He fraternized among the lost because, "It is not the healthy who need a doctor, but the sick," He was saying something very important about His mission...and therefore ours. If He was the doctor, what was the illness? Was it poverty? Was it homelessness? Was it hunger? Was it leprosy and disease? No.

The illness that demanded His cure was sin. His mission was to save people from their sins. Jesus always cared first about the spiritual health of the individual, and second about their physical health. Our mission is certainly amplified and strengthened by our commitment to caring for the physical needs of others. But it is not our urgent mission. To believe it is, is to ignore Jesus' instruction, His example, and the focus of not just His ministry but the one He was commissioning us to fulfill.

One of the most well-known teachings of Jesus was His Parable of the Talents. In the account, Jesus tells of a wealthy landowner who left for a journey. But before going, he called in three of his servants, entrusting each of them with a little bit of his wealth. He gave the first five talents (an amount of gold), the second received two talents, and the last one was given one talent. When the wealthy man returned from his trip, he found that the first servant had invested the five talents and made five more, the second had invested the two talents and made two more, but the final servant had hidden away his talent so it would not be stolen or taken. The final servant returned to the master only what had been given to him. This angered the landowner who confiscated the talent, gave it to the first servant, and had the last one thrown out into the street.

Again, for those who want to live like Jesus, it would be wise to pay attention to the fact that all of His teachings focused on building His spiritual kingdom. Go back to the parable, but recognize that you and I are the servants. And rather than an amount of gold, God has entrusted each of us with various skills, abilities, and gifts (by the way, I should correct myself to note that for some of you, it might be that God has literally blessed you with financial wealth as your "gift").

So what are you using those "talents" for? To make friends? To make peace? To be liked? To live comfortably? Or to save souls from Hell? Only one of those things will please the Master because only one of those things builds His spiritual kingdom and has an eternal return.

The message of false tolerance has paralyzed the church

STRANGERS

today to the point where we regard it as a greater tool of evangelism than confrontation. That is as absurd as it is illogical. I'm wildly intolerant of my own sin. I hate it with everything I am.

A true Christian will never tolerate sin in their own lives. But if Jesus counsels us to love our neighbor as ourselves,[123] it stands to reason that a true Christian will never tolerate sin in another human being. Discernment, tact, sensitivity in knowing how to approach our fellow sinners is one thing; but given that we know what their sin will do to them, we cannot sit idly by as it does.

Typically worldly atheists choose not to understand that perspective, and they join with foolish believers (those "good-cops" we mentioned last chapter) to heap scorn upon real Christians. But sometimes, in rare moments, there are those in the atheist community who get it. They realize that a confrontational Christian is a person acting out of love, not judgment. They also recognize that the "tolerant" Christian earning the world's accolades is in fact a scoundrel and coward.

Penn Jillette is one such atheist, and he deserves to be heard on this issue. In a Big Think video entitled "Why Tolerance is Condescending," Penn rips the hatred of these so-called "tolerant" Christians. Listen up "Good Cop" Christians. This is a masterful wake-up call for all of us:

> "I don't respect people who don't proselytize. I don't respect that at all. If you believe that there's a Heaven and Hell, and people could be going to Hell, or not getting eternal life, or whatever, and you think that, well, it's not really worth telling 'em this because it would make it socially awkward. How much do you have to hate somebody to not proselytize?

19 WHAT IS "LOVING" LIKE JESUS?

How much do you have to hate somebody to believe that everlasting life is possible and not tell them that? I mean, if I believed beyond a shadow of a doubt that a truck was going to hit you and you didn't believe it – if that truck was bearing down on you, there's a certain point where I tackle you. And this is more important than that."[124]

You don't hear me say this often, but Christians could really learn a lesson from this atheist. If we believe that sin exists, if we believe that Hell exists, if we believe that sin leads people to an eternity in Hell, if we believe that Jesus offers the *only* escape from that fate, then we won't "tolerate" anyone's sin.

Instead, we will risk everything: our fame, our fortune, our reputation, our popularity, our job, our family, our friendships... *everything* to expose sin to a world embracing it.

That is our unique nature that makes us strangers. It is our urgent mission that makes us Christians.

STRANGERS

Strategic and Triumphant

STRANGERS

20
YES, ARGUMENT IS GODLY

It's a simple fact that through every era of history, in every culture where it has existed, Christianity and Christians have butted heads with the prevailing spirit of the age. Whenever I point that out to believers here in America, there is an all-too-common eye roll from a select group and either a muttered or implied, "It doesn't have to be that way."

Doesn't it? If Christians are commanded to proselytize and evangelize every corner of the globe (we are), and if the world has a natural tendency to resist being told it is wrong (it does), it is axiomatic that conflict will occur. Yet far too often Christians are apt to believe that confrontation or argument is inherently un-Christlike. Again, do we even know who we serve?

Peruse through the New Testament gospels when you get a chance and notice that you quickly run out of fingers and toes in counting the number of arguments, disagreements and confrontations Jesus had with those He encountered. Yes, Jesus was an arguer. Anyone who is about the Truth will be forced to argue.

When people tell me, "I hate arguing," or "It's not productive to argue," or "No one wins by arguing," I have to fight the urge to stand up on the nearest chair, and scream into a megaphone, "LIAR! COWARD!"

Okay, not really. But as harsh as that would be, it is true. Consider what the person is doing when they say those things to me. They are arguing with me about the nature of arguing.

And here's the crucial question: *why* are they arguing with me? Because they are trying to prove what is true and discard what is wrong. And in order to do that, they must confront what they see as my "wrong" idea. In essence they are validating my original point and proving the essential nature and incredible value of argument. Arguing is a virtue!

Now, of course, I would be remiss not to issue an important Biblical clarification. Useless disputes are not productive and we are told in Scripture to avoid them:

> "Keep reminding God's people of these things.
> Warn them before God against quarreling
> about words; it is of no value, and only ruins
> those who listen."[125]

I can't help but think one of the reasons we are admonished to avoid petty quarrels is because it weakens our credibility to engage useful and productive argument. If we are tagged as mindless contrarians, the world is far less likely to be persuaded by any logical argument we may offer.

Because look at what we're told in the very next verse of that same passage:

> "Do your best to present yourself to God as one

approved, a worker who does not need to be ashamed and who correctly handles the word of truth."[126]

There is a correct way to handle the word of truth. Spoiler alert: it isn't to sit on the truth and be silent about it, allowing the lost and confused to persuade the masses towards folly. If we abandon argument, we've lost our ability to affirm and perpetuate God's Truth to the world.

But, some ask, is anyone actually won over by argument? After all, just look at the various Facebook debates you've ever been a part of to realize how firmly entrenched in our pigheaded positions so many of us are – unwilling to listen to reason, more concerned with public perception of our intellects than genuinely attempting to convince others of our positions. That point is an excellent one to make when discussing *how* we argue. But that wasn't the question. The question was if anyone is ever actually won over by argument.

The Bible tells us:

> "As was his custom, Paul went into the synagogue, and on three Sabbath days he reasoned with them from the Scriptures, explaining and proving that the Messiah had to suffer and rise from the dead. 'This Jesus I am proclaiming to you is the Messiah,' he said. Some of the Jews were persuaded and joined Paul and Silas, as did a large number of God-fearing Greeks and quite a few prominent women."[127]

Paul "reasoned with them." He "explained and proved." And some were "persuaded and joined." So there's our answer. Yes, people are won over by argument.

Others may acknowledge that argument can work, but will

suggest that it isn't the most effective way to "speak" truth. I suppose I'm open to that possibility, but the necessary question to press is, "So what is more effective?" Often times when I ask this, I will get an answer that sounds like, "Well rather than confronting them with my beliefs, I'm just going to love them into the Kingdom."

That's great, but let's get rid of clichés and speak in meaningful terms. What is meant by, "love them into the Kingdom?"

Just being nice to someone doesn't get them to change who they are or what they're doing. To the contrary, it's actually a really good way of convincing them that you think what they're doing is just fine.

Obviously I'm not condemning the idea of loving someone genuinely and without judgment. And obviously I'm not suggesting that doing so is an ineffective tactic to use. But it's not the endgame.

Loving someone is effective not because it brings them into obedience to Christ, but because it establishes the safety and trustworthiness of your friendship. It bolsters your credibility as someone who cares for them, has their best interest in mind, and is a reliable sounding board for their questions.

And that's the key. You love in the hopes that it will one day produce an opportunity for you to answer their serious questions in a Biblical way.

When you do answer them Biblically, it will contradict the way that person is living. Love establishes credibility, believability and confidence in the honesty of your confrontational answers. There is simply no substitute for confrontation in the Christian's playbook. If we possess the only Truth, it's our charge.

S†RANGERS

For their own part, the God-deniers recognize the value of argument. The late Christopher Hitchens was famous for encouraging his fellow atheists,

> "Never be a spectator of unfairness or stupidity. Seek out argument and disputation for their own sake; the grave will allow plenty of time for silence."[128]

Volumes could be written about the logical appeal Hitchens is making to some unseen, unspoken moral authority that determines what is fair and true. It's always an awkward thing for the God-denier to attempt to assume some ultimate, unmovable reference point for morality when their entire worldview is predicated upon subjective relativism.

I suppose if Hitchens was still alive I could "seek out argument" with him over that "stupidity" as he suggests.

But the larger point is that even in the inconsistent worldview of a God-denier, the unique and exclusive value of argument cannot be overestimated. Perhaps, as is their familiar mode of operation, the atheist Hitchens was just borrowing the advice of the Apostle Paul who rallied believers,

> "We demolish arguments and every pretension that sets itself up against the knowledge of God, and we take captive every thought to make it obedient to Christ."[129]

If you're looking for a 21st Century mission statement for American Christians, there it is. Because when dangerous or bizarre ideas, of which we have an overabundance in the United States today, are believed and spread, remember where they lead men. Therefore, ours must be a mission of seek and destroy.

As Hitches said, seek these dangerous and bad ideas out – don't let them lurk in the shadows. Ambassadors of God will expose them and point to a better way.

.

21
WHEN KNOWLEDGE ISN'T ENOUGH

"I'm just not smart enough." If I had a dime for every time I heard a fellow Christian offer this up as a reason why they can't argue or contend for the faith in our culture I would have, well, a lot of dimes. Truthfully this excuse reminds me of Moses' pathetic request to be dismissed from service when God called Him:

> "Moses said to the LORD, 'Pardon your servant, Lord. I have never been eloquent, neither in the past nor since you have spoken to your servant. I am slow of speech and tongue.'"[130]

Can you imagine that scene? The Almighty has appeared in a burning bush, the Creator of the Universe has selected you to go and carry a message to the throne rooms of man, and you respond by saying, "S-s-s-s-orry God, you know I st-st-st-stutter. I c-c-can't do it." Truthfully we should be able to imagine that scene because it's exactly what we do so often. The Son of God appeared to us in the flesh, the Savior of the World has selected us to go and carry a message to the throne rooms of man, and we respond by saying, "Sorry Jesus, I just ain't too bright."

Perhaps before the Lord's anger burns against us as it did against Moses, we should take a look at His response to the would-be deliverer:

> "The LORD said to him, 'Who gave human beings their mouths? Who makes them deaf or mute? Who gives them sight or makes them blind? Is it not I, the LORD? Now go; I will help you speak and will teach you what to say.'"[131]

I have always wondered how Moses saw that conversation going anyway. Did he honestly expect God to extinguish the brush fire instantly after Moses brought up the stuttering thing and say, "Oh. Good point. Hadn't thought that one through had I? Move along and I'll find someone else." Is God really that inept that He makes mistakes in who He calls to carry His truth?

Maybe you need to ask yourself that very question when you're tempted to doubt your own ability to influence and persuade a desperate world. Remember, for all the degrees, book learning and expertise the world has to offer, they lack one thing that you possess: the knowledge of God. Which means that ultimately everything they "know" is futile and fading. Everything you know is eternal and everlasting.

Now I will hasten to add that I'm not advising you just go out and start taking on the great worldly minds of our day without preparation or a plan. Some people do that and end up foolishly causing much damage to the Kingdom of God. Having done no preparation, they march headlong into a hornet's nest of heathens and are fileted for their ignorance, allowing not only themselves but the Word of God to be trampled and trashed.

For as much as I believe we are to be confrontational with our faith, I'm always leery when I hear people say, "I'm not worried about it, God will tell me what to say just like He did Moses." Yes, there is a parallel, but it's not as though God is going to be speaking through a big booming voice into the chambers of your conscience at the precise moment you need a good one-liner to throw at modern pharaohs. It isn't so much that God is going to tell you what to say as it is God has already told you what to say.

He's given us His word. And the degree to which you know it, study it, and have learned it is the degree to which He will be with you when you go out to do battle. If your Bible has a dust-encrusted place on your mantle or bookcase, you're probably as prepared for combat as the long-haired, pudgy seventeen-year-olds who wander into the recruiters office on a Saturday morning. There's some training that needs to be done.

Sometimes people ask me why I'm so confident in voicing my opinions and giving an account for my faith when I know it's going to be challenged. Well to be honest, they're not my opinions. I'm not nearly as confident when I start voicing those. When I'm standing on the authority of God's Word though, I have the utmost assurance that I am speaking Truth. So how do I know the difference between the two?

There's one answer to this: study. In my public school history classroom, students who are really struggling will come to me (sometimes with their parents) and ask for good tips on how to do better. I often tell them that as much as I wish it weren't the case, there's really no secret method or trick to learning the material. It's just study. It's locking yourself in your closet, reading the text out loud if you have to. It's taking notes and going back over the notes. It's reading the same sentence five times if necessary. It's discipline. All that is true for the study of God's Word as well.

If you want to be a person of the Word, a workman who has studied to "show himself approved,"[132] you have to read. Read the Bible. But force yourself to understand what you are reading. Certainly you must read commentaries on the text to gain insight. I also can point to folders full of sermon notes I have taken, some of which have subconsciously worked themselves into sermons I now give. Being a teacher by profession, I quickly figured out my first year in the classroom that you don't really learn a subject until you have to teach it. I applied and apply that principle to many sermon notes that I take: study them and understand them until I reach the point where I'd be confident giving the sermon myself.

I can also advise that the best students are the ones that ask the most questions. Never be afraid to ask questions of God's Word. The key is to actually research them and answer them. That may seem like a silly thing to say, but I can't tell you how often I get emailed questions from believers that could be answered in seconds with a mere Google search (obviously being cautious which sites you trust to provide answers).

I know personally I have no problem at all sharing answers to serious questions believers have, but often times my schedule is swamped and even more often than that, the answers are already articulated in great detail by minds far brighter than my own. As a reference point, bookmark peterheck.com/believe/resources for access to a host of research articles (that I've categorized by degree of difficulty to comprehend) that answer some of the toughest questions about Christianity. There are great apologetics ministries like Answers in Genesis (answersingenesis.org), or the Christian Apologetics and Research Ministry (carm.org), or Glenn Miller's Christian think tank (christianthinktank.com) where you can just type the question you have into the search bar and find excellent, Biblically-based responses.

S+RANGERS

For doctrinal questions, see your church leaders. For apologetic questions, do your research and show yourself approved.

But let me just acknowledge something you may already be thinking. Great resources are helpful to add to our knowledge of God and His Truth. But knowledge alone isn't enough to effectively argue and persuade. How do I know? I'm going to share with you three true stories; friends shared the first two with me as having happened to them, and the third was a personal experience. In each of these instances there were those present who *knew* the truth. But it wasn't enough.

The first occurred at a city council meeting. My friend was a city councilman in a different part of the state, and the council was preparing to enact an ordinance that made divorce filings more difficult to obtain. The testimony from experts as well as the beliefs of a majority of the councilmen confirmed that the epidemic of divorce in our state was doing untold damage particularly to their community. Several of the comments made by citizens were supportive of the measure, many citing the Biblical understanding of marriage-for-life as a worthwhile model.

Then a well-dressed man approached the microphone and directed his questions at my friend. Why are you doing this if not to impose your sense of morality on everybody? Why do you think it's your job in government to promote your values on all of us? My friend encouraged the man to continue with his statement rather than get into a back-and-forth with him. The man wasn't having any of that. He pressed further, "I suppose you're a Jesus follower?" At this, my friend responded affirmatively so as not to fail to give an account of his faith when asked.

The man sneered and asked, "Correct me if I'm wrong but didn't Jesus teach love and respect of people who are different than you? Can you please tell me one place in Scripture where

He told you to tell everyone else how to live?" I truly believe that my friend knew the answer, but was simply dumbfounded by the man's ferocity and anger. He wasn't alone. As I mentioned earlier, the majority of the council were also Christians, but each of them sat back in their chair, undoubtedly thankful that my friend was the one put on the spot.

If you were in that situation, how would you respond? You know the answer, or at least could find the answers to the man's questions. But would you know how to phrase it? How to word it? Would you know the best way to react?

The second situation actually happened on a blind double date. Two of the companions were dating, and they set up two of their friends to go out with them. The man who went as the blind dater is a friend of mine, who explained this was pretty much a doomed experiment from the start.

They went to a bar. My friend doesn't drink. They all started smoking. My friend doesn't smoke. They started talking politics and all were very liberal. My friend may be more conservative than I am. When the topic of discussion turned to abortion, my friend admitted that he knew it wasn't going to end well. After making about a 5 minute, profanity-laced dissertation on why anyone who opposes child-killing in the womb is the devil, his date asked him what he thought about the issue.

To his great credit, he told the truth (to be fair, he admitted that by this point he knew the date wasn't going anywhere anyway). He said something to the effect of, "I believe in God and that He creates every life. And so I think it's wrong that anyone is allowed to end the life of another person." At that precise moment, his date smacked her drink down on the table, stood up and created quite a scene. Most bars and lounges are noisy places, but evidently this one got real quiet, real fast. Apparently coming to the realization that he had been set up on a blind date with Gloria Steinem's daughter, my friend sat

STRANGERS

stunned as his date shouted, "Oh 'heck' no (she didn't say heck). I did not get set up on a date with some Jesus freak Bible banger who is gonna tell me what I can and can't do with my body. You can keep your Philippians out of my fallopians, I'm out of here." And with that, the entire bar broke into applause. My friend said it was the most humiliating moment of his life.

I don't know if he's still friends with the folks who set him up. But I can report that he is happily married to a good Christian woman and they seem quite happy with their Philippian/fallopian arrangement. Now put yourself in his shoes. Would you have known how to handle it or what to say? Suppose it wasn't some surreal scene that was playing out like it was a movie. Suppose it was a family reunion or a Super Bowl party when you were challenged like that. You know the truth, but would you know how to react?

The last situation happened to me after I spoke at a youth event for high school students not long ago. I had been invited to talk about how Christians (and especially Christian teens) should respond to the growing prevalence and acceptance of homosexuality in the culture. After the presentation had ended there was a line of folks that came up to talk. About halfway back I noticed a group of about 6 students all huddled around another and they didn't look happy. When it was their turn I braced myself as one of them spoke up for the group. "Yeah, we are here and brought our friend who is gay." Before I could respond to say that I was glad they came, the girl continued. "We came to this because the title was 'The Truth About Homosexuality' and so we thought you would be talking about how we are to love everyone and not judge them since that's what Jesus said to do."

I interrupted and said that is precisely what my presentation did – it discussed the only loving response to those caught up in same-sex attraction.

At this point the girl who practiced homosexuality spoke

175

up and said in a very harsh, very loud tone, "I'm not caught up in same-sex attraction. I'm gay. It's who I am and it's who God made me to be. Are you telling me I am going to Hell for being who I am?" Trying to diffuse the situation I calmly responded, "I haven't said that anyone is going to Hell. That's not my call. My job is simply to speak God's Truth." At that point, the first girl spoke up again and challenged me (in front of the remaining folks in line, mind you), "So do you say it is God's Truth that she is going to Hell?" I am not going to go into how I answered yet. I simply want to ask you the question how you would respond. You know the truth, but would you know how to react?

Think about those situations and recognize that as believers we are armed with all kinds of apologetic resources and more knowledge than we could ever want or need. You can find the answers and be equipped with the knowledge of God. But I am going to guess that for the vast majority of you reading these pages, you aren't chomping at the bit to be thrown into any of those scenarios I just laid out. You wouldn't be comfortable and you wouldn't be confident.

I have always known my Dad is a smart guy. It seemed like he never stopped going to school or reading. His vocabulary is about 15,000 times that of a normal human being and after watching him just once in his role as a prosecuting attorney, I am beyond convinced that he is wicked smart. He's the kind of lawyer that I am sure accused people don't want to see take their case. But the truth is that his skill in the courtroom is not the result of his knowledge alone. Many people can gather evidence, collect facts, and take statements. But putting it all together? Solving the riddles of a crime scene? Presenting the facts in an understandable way to a jury of far less educated people? That's what makes a smart lawyer a good one.

As a believer, you have the information and knowledge (or can easily get it with discipline and effort). But you lack the confidence to use it or employ it effectively. In the final few chapters, let's start to change that.

22
MOCK THE ENEMY, NOT
THE CAPTIVE

In the final few chapters of this book I am going to work very hard to give you some short, simple, easy methods (that will hopefully stick in your head) that you can use to effectively engage and persuade the lost world around you. To do so, I would be dishonest and wrong to not acknowledge that the vast majority of my inspiration in this regard, as well as the very style of argument I employ personally, comes from one of the most influential and helpful books that has ever been written on the topic.

Gregory Koukl's book called "Tactics" is a must-read for convicted Christians who want to fulfill their mission of urgently speaking truth in a culture that doesn't want to hear it. It's compact and is a quick read – I devoured its roughly 200 pages in one day, and I'm not a speed-reader by any stretch of the imagination. I will do my best to condense and repackage many of the concepts and ideas he elucidates and articulates in far greater detail in his full book. If you're serious about perfecting this skill, buy and read that book.

Before we dig into the actual strategies or methods, I want to be sure to pause and remind you of what you already know. We are right and the world is wrong. And many who are wrong can be very arrogant and very proud about it. We should never shy away from demolishing their views – they are dangerous and leading people to Hell, after all. But always remember the truth that they – the ones who are wrong – are captives. Hugh Hewitt, a man who has engaged in plenty of confrontations over these issues on his nationally syndicated radio show and his post as a CNN contributor, reminds us,

> "It is not the Christian life to wound, embarrass,
> or play one-upsmanship with colleagues,
> friends or even opponents, but it's a common
> vice that anyone can easily fall into."[133]

I know I have made that mistake more times than I care to admit. It became such a focus for me to avoid when I was doing my radio show that I scratched in big letters on the back of my studio notebook the word, "CAPTIVES." I did this just to provide myself a daily reminder what I was doing, what my purpose was, and who I was talking to. We should always be firm, resolute and confident – it will add to the strength of our message. But not allowing it to drift into vanity and arrogance is an important skill I'm still working on. After all, the strength of my ideas rests not in my own head:

> "May I never boast except in the cross of our
> Lord Jesus Christ, through which the world has
> been crucified to me, and I to the world."[134]

All the world offers is vanity and useless, futile chasings

after the wind.[135] Therefore, using our argument to increase our own profile, standing, fame or fortune is waste of eternal proportions. Mocking another person may feel good for a time; it may even elevate our worldly status depending on the degree to which we master the skill. But it is ineffectual and ineffective in building God's Kingdom.

That is not to say there isn't a place for mockery and biting sarcasm. The great former slave-turned-abolitionist Frederick Douglass understood that point. When asked to speak for the 4th of July celebrations in Rochester, NY back in 1852, Douglass accepted the invitation. In his speech, he unleashed a scathing attack on the hypocrisy of a people who would celebrate freedom and independence while simultaneously allowing the yoke of slavery to remain on the backs of its citizens:

> "At a time like this, scorching irony, not
> convincing argument, is needed. O! Had I the
> ability, and could I reach the nation's ear, I
> would, today, pour out a fiery stream of biting
> ridicule, blasting reproach, withering sarcasm,
> and stern rebuke. For it is not light that is
> needed, but fire; it is not the gentle shower, but
> thunder."[136]

Douglass took seriously his Christian role to argue against slavery. And he wisely and judiciously understood that when men have satisfied and contented themselves to live in such utter hypocrisy, argument alone is not as effective as scathing sarcasm and derision. We are certainly living in such times today, and would be wise to utilize the same methods Douglass wielded so effectively. It's *what* we target with the mockery and ridicule that we must be cautious about as believers. Mock Satan. Mock his lies. Don't mock his captives. There's a proverb that applies to this very point. It seems contradictory on the surface, but a deeper look reveals its meaning:

> "Do not answer a fool according to his folly, or

you yourself will be just like him. Answer a fool
according to his folly, or he will be wise in his
own eyes."[137]

See what I mean? It seems like God is telling us in one
breath not to do something that He tells us in the next breath
we better do. A word to the wise: whenever it appears as
though God is contradicting Himself, we're the ones who have
the comprehension problem, not God who has the articulation
problem. The proverb was best explained by, of all people, a
comedian named Thor Ramsey. In a blog post titled, "How is
Sarcasm Helpful" he pointed to an old (dumb) joke you will hear
preachers tell from time to time:

> A wise guy comes up to a Christian in front of a
> crowd and taunts, "So tell me about this Jonah
> guy. How can a man be swallowed by a whale
> and survive for three days?" The Christian
> responds and says, "Well, it was a great fish, not
> necessarily a whale, but to your point: I don't
> know. But I will ask him when I get to heaven."
> The wise guy smirks and says, "What if he isn't
> in heaven?" To which the Christian smirks right
> back and answers, "Then you can ask him."

Clever, huh? But with as tired as that joke may be, Ramsey
points out the great job it does explaining the principle behind
this proverb. And given the vast array of "wise guys" who don't
really have serious inquiries about the Christian faith but are
merely interested in mocking us, we would be wise to
understand it.

> "When you take someone's insincere crack
> about the Christian faith seriously, you become
> the fool & the mocker becomes wise in his own
> eyes. This fool is really scoffing, so Proverbs
> says to answer him according to his wisecrack
> and then he won't be wise in his own eyes."[138]

STRANGERS

That is why sarcasm and biting ridicule can be such an effective tool in the Christian arsenal when used properly. It shows the absurdity of living according to ungodly principles, and the inconsistency of living according to the ever-changing whims of man's fallen intellect. Using it can masterfully turn Christianity from the object of scorn into the only object of any logical consistency. Don't discount the power in that.

And remember, Elijah – who was so holy God didn't even let him suffer physical death but took him into heaven by a chariot of fire – enjoyed the sarcasm. He unleashed a barrage of merciless taunts at the prophets of Baal on Mount Carmel. Why? It most effectively demonstrated the abject powerlessness of yet another religion of man when compared to the one true God. We should not hesitate to do the same. Ramsey demonstrates one example of what it can look like:

> "If the person is only mocking, then by answering an insincere quip with a tongue-in-cheek reply you put the fool in his place. Not that all atheists are insincere in their inquiries, but c'mon… Christopher Hitchens titled his book *god is Not Great: Why Religion Poisons Everything*. Really? Everything? So, you're telling me that if there were no religion that my dining experience at Denny's would be vastly improved? I love omelets, but how do you even enjoy a meal in light of nothingness? It's hard to live as if there is no God, even at Denny's."[139]

Christopher Hitchens is celebrated as one of the great atheist minds of modern times. And here's this comedian who happens to be a Christian, that far fewer people know about, who just dismantled Hitchens' entire thesis with a simple joke about Denny's. Rather than launching into a point-by-point refutation of the accusations Hitchens makes about the faith, Ramsey demonstrates the absurdity and intellectual lack of seriousness in Hitchens' entire premise. And he does it with an omelet reference. Take note, Christians.

I encountered this not long ago when a young attorney for the anti-Christian legal organization called the Freedom From Religion Foundation (the people who sue any Bible, prayer rug, or plastic wise man they can find) sent out a silly tweet to the world. Andrew Seidel is very impressed with his own intellect, and often jokes (at least I think it is a joke) that he can't be beaten in intellectual exchanges. Here was our Twitter conversation, and I'll let you decide. He wrote:

> *Atheist: You should read the bible.*
> *Christian: Is this a trick? Why?*
> *Atheist: Because it's an awful, immoral book*
> *that breeds atheism.*
> *Christian: Then no!*

Now, the natural reaction is to try to argue and point out that the Bible is not an immoral book, but rather the only hope we have of understanding any objective morality at all. But Seidel, like Hitchens, wasn't looking for a serious discussion. He was wanting to mock. So I took a different angle by quoting his Tweet and adding:

> *Evangelistic atheists encouraging people to*
> *read the Bible. Tell me God doesn't have a*
> *great sense of humor.*

I answered the fool according to his folly. He looked silly actually suggesting people read God's word. But, as is often the case with fools, they can't stop – especially when their position has been exposed as foolish. He responded again with:

> *Peter Heck, the road to atheism is paved with*
> *bibles that were actually read cover to cover.*

Now of course that is a ridiculous premise. Seidel himself even brags repeatedly about his practice of either stealing Bibles from hotel rooms that the Gideons have placed, or putting a warning label sticker on them that tells people reading the book might harm them. Which is it, Andrew? Is reading the Bible a threat to a person's health, or is it the best way to produce an atheist? Seidel is so fraught with self-contradiction it would be very difficult to even attempt a rational conversation with him. So I didn't. Instead I just sent back:

> Cool story, bro. I fully support your brilliant strategy.

Fool according to folly. Done, and walk away. Remember that cordiality is to be a goal of ours. When it starts to fall apart, we need to possess the integrity to walk away even if that means we don't get in the last word. In all things, let your ideas offend people, not you.[140]

Now, I don't think for a second that Andrew Seidel is going to be converted because of our exchange. That wasn't my point. My point was preventing Seidel from becoming wise in his own eyes. It was to prevent others who were reading or seeing his anti-Christian screed from being misled or influenced. It was to destroy "every proud notion that sets itself up against the knowledge of God."[141] And that's one of three important points I want to leave you with before we move on. First, never confuse your job with God's job. Jesus was serious when He told us:

> "My sheep listen to my voice; I know them, and they follow me."[142]

But there's something else implied there. Some sheep – or goats if you prefer – are not going to listen to His voice. They'll keep walking around aimlessly, falling off of cliffs and into canyons, or into the clutches of the wolves waiting to devour them. It is not your job, nor is it mine, to bear the weight of converting everyone we confront or argue with. Don't go into the conversation with that being the focus of your thoughts or you will likely be dissuaded from saying what needs to be said.

You are responsible for communicating the Truth clearly and confidently, being faithful to make the gospel known to those who wish to be obedient, and then let God handle the consequences. Results are His responsibility, so don't try to take them out of His capable hands.

Secondly, you do not have to develop a photographic memory or somehow cart around a chip in your brain that has the equivalent of 50 apologetic volumes loaded in it. You are to always be ready to give a reason for the hope that you have,[143] but you are not charged with always being ready to have every answer to every conceivable question that may come your way. No matter how convincing the other side may seem, if Christianity is true (and it is), there will always be a fatal flaw in the thinking, approach, worldview or philosophy of what is being thrown at you. Your job is not to solve every problem or answer every question. It's to answer what you can, and bring the fatal flaw of the opposition to light (more on that soon).

Finally, Gregory Koukl makes a great point in characterizing the nature of various confrontations you and I will deal with given our increasingly hostile culture. He says that they are far less like chess matches where you can prepare, enter with a strategy, and implement it without much surprise.[144] Chess is predicated around intellect and planning. While preparation is indeed important for us Christians, we need to know what we are preparing to face. Koukl says it can be far better described with the analogy of a one-on-one basketball game. In that setting, you know your ultimate objective, but your path to the basket is going to be affected by the movements of your opponent. Is he aggressive, is he patient, does he take risks, is he reserved?

The ability to react to changes and unexpected developments is extremely critical for us as we seek to live out our calling as ambassadors of light amidst the darkness. So let's quickly dig into four short, simple strategies that make that skill much easier to master.

23
STRATEGY I: BE PEYTON MANNING

Probably partially because of my love of American history, but partially because it's such a well written, acted and produced flick, I can't get enough of Mel Gibson's blockbuster movie *The Patriot.* Based loosely off the true history of "The Swamp Fox" Francis Marion during the American Revolution, I will always stop what I'm doing to watch when it comes on TV.

In one of the opening scenes, Gibson's character takes his two younger sons to rescue the oldest brother from a British brigade. As he is positioning the boys behind trees high on the sides of a deep ravine, he reinforces the shooting instruction he had always given them by saying,

"Remember – aim small, miss small."[145]

23 STRATEGY I: BE PEYTON MANNING

Until I went to the shooting range the first time I never understood that line, even though it's a pretty simple concept. If you're aiming to kill a British soldier, you don't aim for his body. That's a large target and if you miss, you are likely to miss him entirely. The idea is that you aim for a small part of him – a button on his red coat. That way, even if you miss your target, you still hit him.

As odd as it may sound, that is the first principle to remember when developing the skills of effective Christian cultural engagement. One of the things I liked about Greg Koukl's book *Tactics* was he came up with clever names for each of the strategies he laid forth. It made it easier to remember. So I've attempted to copy that approach by coming up with four names to commit to memory (they're the names of these four successive chapters if you hadn't figured that out yet). The first is Peyton Manning.

If you want to effectively engage the foreign culture around you, you need to become Peyton Manning – in a couple different ways. Some of the most effective Christian apologists I've known have always counseled that it is important not to set out with any intention of converting others. That may sound weird, but it really isn't. To do so is to "aim big" rather than small.

When a quarterback takes the field to run a play, his objective isn't to win the game. It's to complete a pass. Now, if he successfully completes enough of those passes, and other players do their jobs effectively, the end result may be a team victory. But a good quarterback recognizes his limitations, understands even if he is the most important player on the field, he can't do it all himself. So he controls what he can control and focuses on mastering his job.

Particularly in a polarized culture like American Christians now live in, converting a soul to Christianity usually takes time – at least more than one conversation. It would be wise for us to recognize that fact, adjust our expectations and play our part in what is a much larger operation of the Holy Spirit. And what is "our part?" Let's go back to Manning for a second. I don't know when you are reading this book. But at the time I'm writing it, Peyton Manning, fresh off his retirement still stars in a series of commercials for the insurance company Nationwide. The company has had the jingle "Nationwide is on your side" for years, but it was Peyton Manning whose commercials began putting all sorts of different words to the tune.

> In the supermarket: "That's a first rate queso dip."

> Driving his car: "Haven't been this lost in years."

> Staring at his own bobble head: "Do I really look like this?"

> Eating a sandwich: "Chicken parm you taste so good."

I doubt that I'm the only one who would complain that those dumb commercials and that obnoxious tune have entrenched themselves in my head. I was scurrying down the hallway between classes one day and caught myself singing, "Holy cow I've got to pee" to that stupid jingle. Of course that's the point of any jingle, and Nationwide hit a homerun with the Manning commercials.

That's "our part" that I'm talking about. We are to get in the head of any God-denier or skeptic that we encounter. Plant a seed, if you prefer that analogy. Put something in their mind that will eat at them everywhere they go – even on their way to the bathroom at work.

Koukl reminds us that fruit has to be ripe before it is harvested, and very rarely are the people challenging us anywhere close to being ripe fruit. So rather than try to complete some sort of miraculous germination, fertilization, incubation and harvest all at once, we should seek to simply cultivate the soil around them to aid in the process of their ripening.[146]

Anyone who knows football or ever watched Peyton Manning play would laugh at the notion that the legendary quarterback was a "role player." But that has more to do with the connotations of the word than the truth. Of course he was a role player. In all the years I watched Manning on the field, I never once saw him go out to catch a pass. I never once saw him line up in the defensive backfield to cover a receiver. I never once saw him attempt an extra point or field goal. And on the few occasions he had to run, it was more awkward than watching a three-legged gazelle trying to escape the ravenous lions on National Geographic.

Manning did his part for the team. He knew what his job was, he focused in like a laser on that responsibility and he did it with excellence. If you want to have an effective ministry as a stranger in a strange world, do the same. Plant the seed, leave the person you engage challenged to think about something they hadn't thought about before, cultivate the ripening fruit.

Be Peyton Manning.

24
STRATEGY II: BE PETER FALK

The second strategy in effective cultural engagement for Christians takes us back long before the days of *CSI, NCIS,* or whatever crime drama is currently gracing network or cable television. Beginning in the 1970s, Peter Falk starred in a classic whodunit program called *Columbo.* My grandparents loved the show, and I think I've seen Mom and Dad watching a few episodes through the years as well.

Not until I read Koukl's book had I ever taken the time to watch an episode. But since the majority of *Tactics* revolves around Koukl's *Columbo* method, I figured it would be a good idea. I admit that after seeing the first episode I was again amazed how much better many of those old TV programs were than our current era despite all its technological advantages.

24 STRATEGY II: BE PETER FALK

They seriously don't make shows like that anymore. They try, but they don't come close.

Anyway, the second strategy I would advise is to be Peter Falk. If you've never seen the show, go and Google a picture or two of Agent Columbo and you will see exactly what Koukl describes:

> "The inspector arrives on the scene in complete disarray, his hair an unkempt mop, his trench coat rumpled beyond repair, his cigar wedged tightly between stubby fingers. Columbo's pencil has gone missing again, so his notepad is useless until he bums a pen off a bystander.
>
> To all appearances Columbo is bumbling, inept, and completely harmless. He couldn't think his way out of a wet paper bag, or so it seems."[147]

I can attest after watching a few episodes that this description couldn't be more accurate. Columbo, if anything, is incredibly disarming in his demeanor and appearance. If I was a hardened criminal who had just completed some dastardly deed, the last detective in the world I would fear engaging me would be Agent Columbo.

I think there's a lesson for us there. Our demeanor and approach to the world needs to be disarming as well. When you consider that we are armed with the truth of the universe, with answers the world has nothing but questions about, there is really no reason for us to feel pressure, intensity, or unease in any situation. God plus one is always a majority, and the wisest wisdom of man is dumber than the "folly" of God. If you are saved by the grace of Jesus Christ, no conversation can undo that or weaken your established citizenship in heaven. Don't let this truth breed arrogance – that attitude is far from disarming. It should however instill confidence in you.

STRANGERS

But that isn't the main point of being Peter Falk. Koukl continues, recounting Columbo's famous investigative style:

> "'I got a problem,' he says as he rubs his furrowed brow. 'There's something about this thing that bothers me.' He pauses a moment to ponder his predicament, then turns to his suspect. 'You seem like a very intelligent person. Maybe you can clear it up for me. Do you mind if I ask you a question?'
>
> The first query is innocent enough, and for the moment he seems satisfied. As he turns on his heel to leave, though, he stops himself mid-stride. Something has just occurred to him. He turns back to the scene, raises his index finger and says, 'Just one more thing.'
>
> But 'just one more' question leads to another. And another. Soon they come relentlessly, question after question, to the point of distraction, and ultimately, annoyance."[148]

Now I'm not suggesting that you annoy anyone, but I think Koukl is onto a genius strategy when it comes to Christian engagement with a hostile culture. Questions are our friend. It's a good policy to discipline yourself not to make statements when a question does the job.[149] When I honestly think about it, I can't remember many (if any) questions I've ever been asked that have been hostile or flagrantly aggressive. The ones I might classify that way weren't really questions – they were rhetorical attacks, not honest inquiries.

By its very nature, a question reflects a mind that is inquisitive, interested and intrigued. Simply put, it's much harder to be mad at someone, or to have an uncomfortably hostile exchange with someone like that, than a person who comes across defensive, dangerous, mad, mean, or maligning.

The great benefit of questioning is that you can engage someone without pressure while still controlling the conversation and actually reversing the burden of proof.

Why is this so important? Because what you will find at least 95% of the time you engage a skeptic, God-denier, or cultural revolutionary is that while they are very good at harpooning and trashing your belief system, they don't really know what they believe or why they believe it. That's largely because they've never been asked! The skeptical demands are always placed on Christians these days:

- "Prove God to me and I'll believe in Him."

- "Just because you believe in the Bible doesn't mean you can force everyone else to."

- "Why should tax dollars go to fund an event that leaves non-Christians out?"

- "Why should creation be taught in science class? It's religion."

- "Nobody is asking you to be gay, so why can't you just let people be who they are?"

- "You know you can't legislate morality, don't you?"

- "If you don't like abortion, then don't have one. But who are you to decide for someone else?"

- "Why should we govern ourselves according to the morality of a book written by goat herders from the Bronze Age?"

And the list goes on and on and on. To effectively engage such a hostile culture, we Christians need to learn how to reverse this scrutiny back onto the skeptics. Rather than attempting to "prove Christianity" every time we have a discussion, it is far more reasonable and responsible to "aim small" and first get the skeptic thinking about his alternatives. You do that through questions.

If King Solomon is right that there is "nothing new under the sun"[150] then we aren't dealing with original thinkers. We are encountering people who simply parrot what they've heard or read. They may possess an antipathy towards Christianity based on a personal experience or on the perception of the faith they've been given. But they've never actually been forced to think through their own beliefs. Remember that the world is full of what Paul called "fine sounding arguments,"[151] so it is not surprising that many who are untethered to the foundational truths of Christianity have been seduced by them. When you ask them to clarify what they believe, they are undone.

For instance, when challenged by someone that, "Believing in God is just irrational," I am tempted to respond by saying, "Actually, believing in magical exploding fairy dust that turns into everything is what is irrational." I admit that it's possible I have even retorted with that a time or two. Oops. The reason I say oops isn't because it's untrue. It's because it is a far less effective strategy since it's an aggressive attack that immediately puts the other individual on the defensive. What I've always received when I say that is not, "You know what, you're right. Tell me more about God." It's always a web link to BigBang.com or some atheist website that will provide all the scientific "proof" I could possibly want.

So what's a better strategy? Don't be Peter Heck. Be Peter Falk. When someone says that belief in God is irrational, ask them why. "Help me understand what part of God you find to be irrational." That's a great question to ask because ultimately there's nothing irrational about believing in God. The skeptic will soon discover that through your "helpful" questions. Belief in the Big Bang *still* requires something to instigate or initiate the "bang," doesn't it? Complex DNA is best explained by a complex author, is it not? Unwritten moral law that we all seem to understand demands a lawgiver, right? Questions will reveal all of these things and challenge the skeptic in a way they've never been challenged before.

If nothing else, they will become far less hostile towards the answers you are offering when they recognize that they really don't have all the answers themselves. Now, inevitably you will encounter someone hardened and pigheaded about their own intellect and ability to understand all the secrets of the universe apart from God's authority. You will quickly figure that out in the course of your questions. Cordially ending the conversation is more than acceptable at that point, but it's not always the wisest decision. First of all, remember your objective is to get in their head and leave them with something to think about. Don't depart until that has been accomplished. And secondly, recognize that the Holy Spirit may not be working on the person you're even talking to, but rather someone who is watching the conversation. When it's an exchange on Facebook or some online entity, you might not ever even know it.

I'll give you one example of this. Not long ago I published a story dealing with the cultural turmoil that would unfold as a result of "un-defining" the institutions of marriage and family (so that alternative partnerships and unions besides God's monogamous man/woman design could be included). A college professor hopped on to challenge me and wrote:

> Marriage is a legal contract between two consenting individuals who agree to the rights and responsibilities of said contract. It has nothing to do with religion. Same-sex marriage has been present since your "biblical times". It is not borrowing a title. It is not anything other than a legal contract between two consenting individuals. Heterosexuality does not own the term "Marriage", and neither does any religion.

Now, understanding the lifestyle choices of this particular professor, and also having been subject to some personal attacks from her in the past, I was well aware that barring some miracle of God, she was not likely to have her mind changed by my words. But I didn't know who else was reading and being influenced by her "fine sounding argument." So I responded:

> *Why two? Are you making a moral condemnation of those who are born polyamorous? Why shouldn't they get to experience the happiness of marriage that you are allowed to experience? And two consenting individuals would include incestuous right? Tell me you believe in true marriage equality and aren't forbidding someone to love who they want to love based on your own moral code.*

Notice the questions. They were placed there with the desire to make her (or really make others who were inclined to agree with her) think through the implications of their publicly held positions. She wasn't interested in doing that personally, but as you will soon see, her responses were going to leave some giant question marks for those who had perhaps thought they originally agreed with her. Here was how the conversation unfolded:

> *Prof: Peter, The reason it is currently between two people is the same reason you cannot sell the exact same car to three complete strangers who are not jointly purchasing said vehicle. I would also like to point out that you know nothing of what constitutes polyamory if you are trying to suggest this sexuality is being harmed by the current legal status of marriage. As for incestuous marriage, if that is what you are wanting, you are more than welcome to work toward getting it acknowledged by law. Currently, it is illegal due to historical evidence of birth defects and, in some cases, due to the fact that it cannot be accomplished with*

consent. Nice try. Try harder next time.

Me: Nonsense. If three parties wish to enter a contractual agreement, they are allowed to do so. But not marriage. Why? Why do you oppose that? And I am aware of the reasons incestuous marriage has been forbidden historically. I'm curious whether you think the law should forbid it. After all, [name redacted], as homosexual activists have told us repeatedly, marriage isn't about procreation. So should these consenting adults be legally forbidden to marry?

Prof: Three unique parties are not allowed to enter a contractual agreement in which only two parties can be the only ones to benefit. When we begin to analyze the rights and responsibilities of a marriage, those of us who understand the legal details of marriage, recognize that legal issues such as SSDB, taxes, estate laws, medicolegal standing, and survivorship must be first negotiated before polygamy can be legalized. But, why not let it. Who am I to stand in the way of consenting adults entering a committed and honest relationship. I noticed you breezed right past consent when dealing with incestuous relationships. Don't you believe a relationship should be entered into through consent? Why the fixation on incest, pedophilia, and sex? It seems you spend an awful lot of your time fixated on LGBTQ sexuality. In fact, you spend more time thinking about what is going on in my bedroom than I do. Don't you find that a little disturbing you are more interested in other people's sex lives than is actually healthy? BTW, I understand why you throw out these

false narratives, distractions, and hyperboles.
You have no leg to stand on, and no
understanding of which you are trying to speak.
That's ok. We understand. We were once where
you are now.

This is a good place to stop for a second and point out what is unfolding in this conversation, and what is likely to happen in many of yours. Do not be surprised, angry, hurt or deterred when personal attacks make an appearance in the discussion. They are a sign that the other person is growing very uncomfortable with the way things are going for them – that's a good thing! Yes, I'm telling you that you should actually feel more confident when you start getting called names (or in this case, have your opponent allege that you are some sort of kinky sex freak).

Notice that the professor was forced to acknowledge something she no doubt did not want to acknowledge – that she believed in legalizing polygamy. That's why the longer you can bear personal insults or taunts, ignore them, and stay focused, the better. Your calm demeanor contrasted with their aggression only goes to further your credibility and weaken theirs.

> *Me: Hi [name redacted], thank you for*
> *acknowledging that you believe in legalized*
> *polygamy. But are you seriously suggesting that*
> *there are no incestuous relationships that are*
> *consensual? That's silly. So for those that are,*
> *do you believe in legalized incestuous*
> *marriage?*

Another quick point: please notice the length of her comments compared to mine. This isn't easy for me because by nature I am very wordy (as becomes evident as the conversation continues). But I am staying focused and to the point. She is beginning to ramble and argue everything but the kitchen sink. She is even attempting to be Peter Falk in an undisciplined way – throwing out questions as a means to get us going down a rabbit hole where she would be more comfortable. In this particular discussion, the professor even started bringing up my profession as a high school teacher, alleging that I could not possibly provide an "equal education" to all of my students if I felt LGBT behavior was sinful.

This was the one moment when I allowed myself to go off topic. This professor seemed new to my comment section so I thought perhaps she was not aware of the rules I have established. And notice what happened the moment I indulged her off-topic question and answered it:

> *Me: [Name redacted] as I've stated numerous times on here, I work very hard to separate the two professional spheres of my life. There has never been a student in my classroom that I haven't loved and treated in the most Christ-like way I know how. This is not a forum to discuss my role in the classroom, so we're done discussing the topic.*

> *Meanwhile, perhaps you could answer the question. You have affirmed that you believe in legalized polygamy. Do you believe in legalized incest for consenting couples?*

> *Prof: Let me show you how a real educator does it, Pete. I proudly and gladly provide all my students with the same high quality and equal education regardless of race, ethnicity, nationality, sex, gender, sexual orientation, gender identity, religion, creed, affiliation, and ability. I am proud to recognize the diversity of the students in my classroom, and I am proud to provide them an educational learning environment that fosters growth, learning, and*

the life skills to prepare them to meet all their goals and dreams. It would never occur to me to treat any student differently or to discriminate against any student.

That's how a real educator answers the question.

The moment I allowed distraction to enter the conversation, even as a sign of goodwill towards her, she jumped at it in order to escape the uncomfortable direction things were going. That's why when it is at all possible, ignore superfluous distractions like taunts and unrelated queries, and keep driving your questions. Here's how our conversation ended:

Me: It is patently obvious to anyone reading this that you are intentionally avoiding answering the question that is actually germane to the post. You have acknowledged you believe in legalized polygamy. I would assume you are embarrassed by that admission. You should be.

You now also realize that you are stuck regarding incest. You know it is inappropriate and immoral, but your own publicly professed definition of bigotry prevents you from forbidding it lest you become the bigot. So you won't acknowledge that given your publicly stated positions, you would be forced to agree with legalized incest for consenting adults. You should also be embarrassed by that.

What these questions have revealed (and you know this because you're an educated person) is that everyone - not just radical right wing Christians - have moral codes that they seek to enact through legislation. You have moral boundaries for what we call marriage just as much as I do. But you want to pretend that is not the case so you can carry on with your character assassination of those you disagree with. It's transparent and extremely unprofessional. But it is par for the course with the LGBT lobby.

In an effort to deflect the conversation from this embarrassing reality, you have attempted multiple times to suggest that I somehow deprive certain students in my classroom of an equal education (which is absurd)... I will say one more time that I am not going to discuss my role as a teacher here. This is a forum for my profession as a political columnist and social commentator/speaker. I have posted thoughts that you are more than free to discuss. But you are not more than free to attempt to save face when embarrassed by diverting the conversation away from the topic and onto something else.

Prof: [A]llowing marriage equality for same-sex couples does not "destroy the institution of marriage." In fact, it strengthens marriage as it demonstrates the importance of marriage to a society. I have never said incestuous marriage should be allowed, it violates the construct of consent. So does this inane argument that you all seem to make about animals and inanimate objects. Again, marriage is the VOLUNTARY, LEGAL CONTRACT made between two CONSENTING ADULTS. A car cannot consent. In a parent-child relationship, a child (even as an adult) cannot consent to a marriage. Just to tackle the rest of the stupidity of the inane arguments of the extremist religious reich wing... No, you cannot marry your dog, your toaster, a dead person, a deity, a building, a business, or someone who refuses to marry you. The reason is not bigotry, but lack of consent. That is the law, and NO LGBTQ+ ACTIVISTS are attempting to remove consent from the law.

Me: Hey [name redacted], a couple questions. First of all, what about consensual incestuous relationships? You haven't answered that yet, and they do exist. Are you willing to deny them the right to be happy? Isn't that bigoted? We can get into your arbitrary rules of consent predicated upon your own moral code later. But for now, perhaps you could tell us if you believe in marriage rights for consenting incestuous couples as you do for polygamy?

Prof: I will answer your questions when you man up and answer the question I asked you first. Come on, man up.

Me: I asked you this question in my very first post to you. You have danced and dodged it this whole exchange. You've called names and intimated ridiculous things you know nothing about all in an attempt to deflect. To be honest, you've been caught in your inconsistency and that's all I cared about - giving you something to think about when you hurl your pejoratives around. You are guilty of violating your own standards of "decency." Besides I've already answered your question when I said that the idea I wouldn't provide equal respect and a well-rounded educational experience to certain students was "absurd." Now please respect my rules for this page, which include keeping my school and teaching profession separate. If you can't, go post elsewhere.

Prof: So, if you are giving LGBTQ+ students an equal education, then you don't think being gay is a sin. Am I right?

And you are the one fixated on incest and non-consensual relationships. I oppose all relationships that are non-consensual, as it is a form of rape.

Me: That your only apparent barometer for measuring the morality and appropriateness of a sexual relationship is "consent" is beyond irresponsible and foolish.

In terms of your question, I have to hand it to you that it may be the most logically impaired deduction I have ever seen attempted on this page.

I have asked you and told you multiple times now what the rules are and you have refused to respect them. So be it. This will be the last post on this thread.[152]

The logically impaired deduction I was referring to was the attempted implication that if I believe any particular student is a "sinner" I can't possibly provide them an equal education. Given that *every* Christian believes that *every* person is a sinner of some sort, the logical deduction from this professor's reasoning would mean that no Christian could possibly offer *any* student an "equal education." It's tough to characterize how confused and bizarre that thinking is.

Incidentally, there were two other individuals who would interject comments at times that would distract the flow of the conversation. For the sake of space, I have edited those out. However, if you wish to see the entire conversation it is available at the footnote provided (I've learned whenever you edit something, even for the sake of brevity, keeping a full copy of the entire exchange is imperative to avoid accusations of selective editing).

Again, hopefully this one online conversation demonstrates that the process of being Peter Falk is never a guarantee that you will convert the other person. It's not a guarantee that things will always go exactly as planned. But it is a demonstration that being able to adjust to a variety of distraction attempts, personal insults, and red herrings with focus and calmness takes the pressure off you almost entirely, reverses the burden of proof on the accuser, and hopefully causes those watching from a distance to consider things they hadn't thought of previously. It should also be a reminder that not everyone you encounter will leave being your best friend. Better that be the result than they leave never having heard the truth.

To be sure, being Peter Falk is a perfect strategy for the most awkward situations. Remember the LGBT girl that confronted me at the youth event I wrote about in Chapter 21? A friend of the girl loudly demanded that I answer the question, "So do you say it is God's Truth that she is going to Hell?" Luckily, I had read Koukl's *Tactics* where he addresses a very similar challenge.

My response was to ask the students gathered in that crowd if they believe there's right and wrong. A question. They all agreed there was such a thing as right and wrong. I then asked them if they believe that wrong things deserve to be punished. A question. They all agreed that to some degree all wrong things deserve to be punished. I then asked them if they had ever done anything wrong. A question. They all agreed that they had. I told them I had too – I'd done a number of things wrong and that I thought I deserved to be punished for them. I asked them if they thought they deserved to be punished for the things they had done wrong. A question. They agreed that they did.

Notice how by the Peter Falk strategy I went from being put on the spot about whether I would condemn a girl to Hell for her gay lifestyle to having unanimous agreement amongst the entire group that we *all* deserved to be punished! And that's when the gospel message fits so perfectly:

God is perfectly holy. He allows nothing into His presence that isn't perfect. It's why He kicked Adam and Eve out of the Garden. It's why in the Old Testament the Hebrews had to conduct unblemished sacrifices to cover over their sins. And it's why God's ultimate plan to save us was to offer His own perfect Lamb as a once-for-all sacrifice for what we'd done wrong and would do wrong.

I started ignoring all of the other kids in that group and stared right at the young lady who told me she was gay. And I said to her, "I want you to know that my moral crimes against God are every bit as bad as yours. He tells me not to do things that I did and still struggle not to do. He tells you the same. I can promise you that where you spend eternity is nobody's choice but your own. If you accept that perfect sacrifice of Christ, which means repenting of those things you know He's told us not to do, and try everyday to walk in newness of life with Him, you follow His plan for salvation, then you will be in heaven one day with me. Not because of anything I did or you did to earn it. But because of what He did for us." I told her I would be praying for her and asked her if she would pray for me. That's how we left it.

Be Peter Falk.

25
STRATEGY III: BE GEORGE FEENY

I may not have grown up in the era of *Columbo*, but I can tell you all you want to know about a TV show called *Boy Meets World*. It was a Disney/ABC program that followed the childhood-to-college years of Cory Matthews, his family, his girlfriend Topanga and his friend Shawn.

It was a staple in my must-see TV list of shows. The sitcom featured a handful of different teachers at Cory's school, but without question, Mr. George Feeny was the most recognizable. Given the adoration fans had for Feeny's character, the writers wisely wrote him in as Cory's next door neighbor as well, increasing the amount of screen time he received.

On more than a few occasions, I seem to remember Feeny would hammer "Mr. Matthews" for not "showing his work." As most of the clever high school students I deal with daily still attempt to pull off, Cory would have merely copied his answers out of the back of the book and turned them in. Feeny would have none of it. If you couldn't demonstrate how you arrived at an answer, your answer wasn't good enough for Feeny.

The third strategy in Christian cultural engagement is to be George Feeny. We need to copy and emulate that mindset as we engage those hostile to Christian thinking. When someone hurls out an accusation towards you or about our faith, it is highly likely that they have merely copied their answer out of the back of the book. That is, they have read it or heard it somewhere, know it is an alternative to the Christian explanation, and so they merely parrot it.

Big Bang proponents offer a great example of this. When pressed, people who want to reject the moral accountability that comes from the existence of a Supreme Creator need to find an alternative explanation for the existence of the universe. The easiest thing to espouse is, "I believe in the scientific explanation known as the Big Bang."

That's a position that Peter Falk may flush out by asking a question, but it's an answer that has likely been copied out of the back of the book. Peter Falk needs to transition into George Feeny and ask the all-important follow-up: "Oh, okay. I guess I figured if you didn't believe in intentional design that you believed in the Big Bang, but I meant why? What makes the Big Bang theory so much more reasonable to you?"

When you ask that (and I have), you are likely to get a mixed bag of scientific terms, claims to various pieces of data, and a general statement that the scientific evidence concludes that is what happened. But that isn't true at all. The notion of a cosmic singularity is *assumed* by those who want philosophical answers that don't include God. The "evidence" is then interpreted to *fit* the assumption. It's a cart-before-the-horse problem. Same thing goes for Darwinism. Fossils and evidence are interpreted in a way that fits the Darwinian assumption. But the assumption was made before the evidence was found. The same evidence can fit nicely into a far different assumption – one of intentional design – as we have found.

If you doubt that, take a look at one of the most astounding admissions I have ever seen from the so-called "scientific community." Harvard Genetics Professor Richard Lewontin writes openly,

> "Our willingness to accept scientific claims that are against common sense is the key to an understanding of the real struggle between science and the supernatural. We take the side of science in spite of the patent absurdity of some of its constructs."[153]

Are you getting that? The odds of all the immaculate design we see around us coming purely by chance are a mathematical impossibility. But Lewontin is admitting that scientists accept that "absurdity" anyway. And why? He continues:

> "...because we have a *prior* commitment, a commitment to materialism. It is not that the methods and institutions of science somehow compel us to accept a material explanation of the phenomenal world, but, on the contrary, that we are forced by our a priori (before the fact) adherence to material causes to create an apparatus of investigation and a set of concepts that produce material explanations, no matter how counterintuitive, no matter how mystifying to the uninitiated."[154] (emphasis added)

This is stunningly honest. Lewontin is saying in essence, "We decide beforehand that we don't want the answer to our universe to be God or anything supernatural that we can't explain. So we accept absurd notions like the Big Bang, life arising from non-life, macro-evolution and everything else, not because the evidence compels us to, but because we *have* to accept it given our assumptions. And we do that no matter how silly the story we are telling may become." Why? Check out this final line:

> "Moreover, that materialism is absolute, for we cannot allow a Divine Foot in the door."[155]

This is the kind of debate-altering, mind-opening discovery you will find when George Feeny shows up in your conversation.

As Koukl affirms, you will likely be shocked how many who challenge your beliefs are unprepared to defend their own.[156] He suggests not letting them off the hook but instead utilizing the show-your-work demand in a principle he calls "A House Without Walls":

> "Think of an argument like a simple house, a roof supported by walls. The roof is the conclusion, and the walls are the supporting ideas. By testing the walls, we can see if they are strong enough to keep the roof from tumbling down...
>
> Some arguments are not really arguments at all. Many people try to build their roof right on the ground. Instead of erecting solid walls (the supporting ideas that hold the conclusion up), they simply make assertions and then pound the podium – or verbally pound you...
>
> Roofs are useless when they are on the ground. No one can live in a house without walls. In the same way, an assertion without evidence is not very useful...

STRANGERS

> Your job is to recognize when the roof is lying
> flat on the ground and simply point it out.
> Don't let someone flatten you by dropping a
> roof on your head. Make him build walls
> underneath his roof. Ask him for reasons or
> facts to support his conclusions."[157]

It may well be that the person you're talking to has no idea
that brilliant intellects like Lewontin have acknowledged that
the "scientific" view of these great philosophical questions of
life is built on an assumption – or blind faith. When you
become George Feeny and start asking him to reveal his walls,
he may be as surprised as you to discover his roof is laying on
the ground.

As I mentioned last chapter, in our culture, God-deniers
are almost never expected to defend their beliefs. Yes, it's
annoying, but it's an opportunity. Here's how I became Feeny in
a recent conversation with an atheist online after he challenged
me that my views were evil:

> Me: What is evil? (I'm asking for a definition, not
> examples) And how do you know it's evil?

> Him: Do you think without God, you could not
> distinguish between what is good or evil, Peter?

> Me: I'm not sure why you aren't answering my
> question, [name redacted]. You made an
> explicit statement, "evil exists." You should be
> able to explain that, shouldn't you?

> Him: Let's us (sic) play this game. Evil is the
> immoral actions to inflict harm on someone for
> any reason.

> Me: I'm not playing a game. I'm trying to
> understand your thinking. And I appreciate you
> making an attempt, but you didn't answer the

question. Evil is immoral acts, obviously. I'm curious how you define what is moral and immoral? What is your standard or measuring rod? How do you KNOW what evil is? Have you ever thought deeply about that question and examined it from the perspective of what you claim to believe?

Him: Our morality and ideas of evil can be shaped in a few ways. The first being that social behavior or society shapes our views on evil and immorality or morality itself and I think we can agree on that.

We also have the ability to reason, to be able to think about the actions that are considered to be evil like rape, murder, torture and so on and come to the conclusion that they are harmful to the people they are being committed on.

I find it interesting that the basis of religious people's morality only comes from the fear of being punished if they commit such acts from a God who demands you worship him for entry into a kingdom where he will love you forever.

Our morality has come from man this entire time even if you were to say you get it from the bible, man wrote the bible.

Me: Thanks [name redacted]. The reason I re-asked the question is because you essentially used the defined word in the definition. You said that "evil" is when people commit "evil acts." That doesn't answer the question.

Your second response was far more helpful. It appears your answer on "what is evil" and "how do we know what evil is" is, at its heart, quite subjective.

Society shapes our views of evil, and we use our "reason" to decide what we think evil is. Am I fairly stating your definition? I am not trying to put words in your mouth.

You COULD be saying that we use our "reason" to determine some ultimate, unchanging absolute moral law that exists for all people, in all times, in all places.

But I don't think that's what you're saying. I think you are saying we subjectively determine what we believe evil "should" be for our own time.

Just please clarify that so I don't question or argue against something you're not saying. I promise all I am doing here is just collecting information to better understand you. Do you agree that your definition of evil is subjective?

Him: Do you think morality could not exist without God, Peter? Do you believe people could not distinguish between good and evil on their own?

Me: I don't know why you are uncomfortable answering questions about your own beliefs, [name redacted]. Have you not spent as much time thinking through them as you have coming up with reasons why God is silly?

You have given me an answer about what evil is that is subjective. Would you or would you not agree with that?

My position on evil is that it is certainly objective – unchanging. And that we know what evil is based off of the revelation and the reason that God – the Moral Lawgiver – has given us. He is the standard of good.

Anything that contradicts His character, commands, or will, is bad. That is a very objective standard. To discover that "natural law," He has given us both His revelation (Scripture) and our reason. Using the two in concert, we discover Moral Law and apply it.

Discovering the Moral Law that delineates between good and evil is not the same as "determining" it for ourselves. That seems to be your understanding of evil. Am I right?

Him: Your (sic) saying that your ideas are objective rather than subjective on evil is the same as mine. I can clearly define what evil is but someone could definitely not agree with us or totally see it differently. Our differences (sic) is that you rely on God for your goodness and to recognize evil and I do not need that.

Me: That's a confusing response and I admit I don't follow it. My position is that Moral Law is unchanging through time, regardless of circumstance. I can know that because God, the Moral Lawgiver, has told us as much.

Your position is that if society wills it, the definition of what is evil can be altered. Those two positions are not compatible.

Further, you enjoy mocking the notion that I "need" God or concept of eternal punishment to make me do right. Do you feel similarly about worldly authority? Do you "need" a government in place to prevent you from breaking the law? It's a bizarre line of reasoning to say the least. The concept of eternal justice should not be any less reasonable than the concept of earthly justice it would seem. Why do you mock one but not the other.

Him: We can go our separate ways on this, you will never convince me that God is real, that the God you worship is a powerful, merciful God when he is the exact opposite. You were not born with the belief in God, you were taught to believe in God to be a good little child or else and surprisingly it works.

If you believe that is great but don't act like a fool and try to convince others they are terrible people, that is when it annoys me.

Again, just like with the professor in the last chapter, it is apparent that this guy didn't change his mind because of our conversation. But you can tell from his final response that he was left acknowledging there is a hole in his thinking. He may not want to fill it with God and he may refuse to do so. But it was exposed. That's our job. As former Ambassador Alan Keyes has said,

> "It is not for us to calculate our victory or fear our defeat, but to do our duty and leave the rest in God's hands."[158]

Part of our duty, it seems, is to be George Feeny. In your effort to do so, remember some of these great questions to put in your arsenal: "How did you come to that view?" or "I'm not sure I follow, can you help me out in understanding how that makes sense?" When you become Feeny it is no longer your job to defeat their claim, it is their job to defend it. And make sure that they do it with reasons (or "walls" as Koukl would say).

The moment my Facebook friend above revealed his walls (or lack thereof), it was then much easier for me to apply the three P's of drawing a conclusion: possible, plausible, probable. Once everyone's "walls" and reasoning have been revealed, the logical thing to do is to compare which one holds its roof up better. That means we don't just determine if something is possible. We can determine which one is more plausible and probable to be right.

For instance, let's suppose that a woman named Janet ends up murdered. Barry is arrested for the crime. Now, I didn't see it happen myself, so can I be *absolutely* certain that he did it? No.

But there are three eyewitnesses that saw him do it. DNA evidence gathered by the police puts him at the scene, mixed in the victim's blood, and holding the murder weapon. He also had extreme financial and emotional motive to commit the crime. So I come to an informed conclusion that says he did it. The roof of my house is now that Barry killed Janet.

But someone else says he didn't do it. They have a different theory. They believe that an alien came, abducted Barry, took him back to the mothership where they copied his DNA and form, embedded it into one of their own, sent the alien version of Barry to the earth as an exact replica (all while the real Barry was in an inter-galactic coma), the alien Barry committed the crime framing the real Barry, returned to the mothership, and sent the real Barry back to earth to face the punishment.

That's his roof. Looking at the walls of our houses, is it possible that his is right? I suppose if you want to be technical, it is within the realm of universal possibility. But once we examine the walls of our theories, which one is more plausible? Which one is more probable? What is the best answer?

This is the point we need to press towards in our conversation with the dying culture around us. They are confused and lost. They have no basis to explain morality, which means they have no basis to uphold it long-term. They have no understanding of the purpose of our existence. We need to press to the point of exposing their walls so we can rationally make the case that our roof is more reliable than theirs.

The strategy of being George Feeny should not be misunderstood as dodging or attempting to avoid defending our own faith or beliefs. As Koukl says repeatedly, when we state our beliefs, we bear the burden of proof. But when others state theirs (as they will do when Peter Falk gets involved), they bear the burden of proof.

Too often Christians in America allow our critics to simply live off their skepticism. Years ago, the head of the apologetics ministry AiG, Ken Ham, had a much publicized, widely-viewed debate with former atheist TV host Bill Nye. I thought the debate was good and productive, but I was disappointed with the chosen topic both sides agreed upon for the debate.

It was, "Is Creation a Viable Model of Origins." Notice from the start who is immediately on the defensive. Now, to be fair to Ham, I'm sure that Nye demanded this be the topic if he was going to participate. But recognize it wasn't "Is Molecules to Man Evolution a Viable Model for Life" or "Is the Big Bang a Viable Model of Origins." Can you imagine what would be revealed to a watching world if such a concept was actually debated?

Skeptics of Christianity are almost never expected to defend their theories or beliefs in American culture. That's by design, but needs to change. Being George Feeny will help change it.

26
STRATEGY IV: BE LARRY BIRD

Perhaps you'll be pleased to know that if you made it this far, these last two chapters are going to be a breeze. They will compete with one another to see who can be shorter and more to the point.

The final strategy I would heartily suggest for Christian "strangers" looking to properly fulfill their Christ-commissioned duty as ambassadors of God in a lost and depraved culture would be this: be Larry Bird.

About the time I was in junior high school, I was convinced that God's plan for my life involved a career in the NBA. Seriously…in junior high I was still believing that. If you want proof, head out to my parents' house. In the backyard by the garden and burn pile, you will see a large concrete slab that is now overgrown. There's a big metal post that has nothing but a rim sticking off the end of it, as the backboard rotted away sometime in the last couple decades.

If you push back the brush in the northwest corner of the slab, you will see my initials PWH carved into the concrete. And right next to them, in much smaller letters (so as not to be visible by anyone who would notice and mock me) are the initials NBA. My goal, obviously, was to shock everyone by making it to the big leagues, and then when I led my team to the finals and the NBA on NBC did a special on me, they could come out and film the Peter Heck training grounds. Seriously, it's an arrow in the quiver of my enemies that I have always had a streak of delusion about myself.

But shortly after those initials were carved, I went to a basketball camp where one of the coaches told us that the great Indiana basketball legend Larry Bird had committed himself to waking up at the crack of dawn every day. He would go out to the basketball goal on his barn and shoot 100 free throws every morning. It was his discipline and work ethic that led him to the heights of basketball glory.

That's all I needed to hear. Who knew that making it to the NBA required only that a person go out and shoot 100 free throws every day. I would have guessed there was natural talent and ability, genetics, proper coaching, genetics, good diet, genetics, a particular skill set, and genetics that all factored in. But no...just 100 free throws! When I got home from that camp I had my mom buy a big white poster board that I made into a calendar chart to keep track of how many I made each day. The poster board was big enough that I was able to map out not just the summer, but well into the fall and winter also. I will have you know I made it a good three weeks into the chart before I started missing some mornings. Then weeks. The chart was taken down to spare myself embarrassment sometime around August.

S†RANGERS

Obviously there are many more factors into having a career like Larry Bird's than just 100 free throws a day. To be honest, I don't even know if that story about Bird is true. But I do know that when it comes to being an effective Christian ambassador in the culture, ready to engage the false notions that set themselves up against the knowledge of God, ready to demolish the foolish teachings that are dragging men down toward the pit of eternal Hell, there is no substitute for discipline.

We must be relentless in our study of the Word of God, yes. But more than that. If you want to be effective in communicating with the culture around you, you have to practice your application of the knowledge of God. That means doing it. Repeatedly. I will admit to something that you may find silly, although I am guessing I am not the only one that does this.

I listen to a lot of talk radio where these cultural issues and topics are debated and discussed. Almost every time I do, I end up hearing something that I challenge myself to respond to. I will turn the radio down after the host or a caller has made a point or asked a question, and I will pretend that I am there talking to them. I answer them – going into full detail and using Manning, Falk and Feeny.

I try to hone that same skill on Facebook and other forms of social media. Sometimes I'm more successful than others. I started a daily blog where I am forging arguments and defending them – and many times where I am writing Christian rebuttals and responses to the things other secular and ungodly commentators have written or said. Relentless. Determined. Constant.

There are so many great ways to learn these tactics and strategies. I've started doing three-day retreats for Christian teenagers (16-19) who are preparing to leave home and go to college or into the workforce. Unlike most church camps or conferences, our intent is not to entertain them, or even to introduce them to the gospel. It is specifically designed for churched, committed Christian young people, and is a retreat aimed at training them how not just to defend their faith in a hostile environment, but to turn the tables and wage an offensive campaign for truth. You can find out more information on these 414 Retreats (reference to Esther 4:14) on our website: peterheck.com/414.

We've even started a video training series for anyone at peterheck.com. If you go there and sign up for our mailing list, every so often you will receive a series of four to six short videos (usually no more than a couple minutes long) right to your inbox that cover how to talk to the world as a Christian about various topics. We've gotten great feedback from subscribers and would love to have you as part of the group. I try to respond individually to all follow-up questions that come to me from those videos, giving whatever expertise I can.

And there are so many other great Christian ministries that train and teach these skills, like Answers in Genesis, Stand to Reason (Koukl's organization), Ravi Zacharias International Ministries, and a host of others. The internet certainly brings with it great temptations and great evil. But it also makes Biblical apologetic and engagement training so much more accessible and affordable than it has ever been before.

If you want to change your world, forget the free throw chart, but be Larry Bird.

27
BE A FOOL

One of the things those closest to me are so tired of hearing me say is that we are living in the midst of a Queen Esther moment. Many of you probably know the story of Hadassah the Jew-turned-Esther the Queen. Torn from her family after being selected in nothing short of a beauty pageant held by King Xerxes in his search for a new wife, this young woman became the pivotal figure that God used to rescue His people from the hand of their enemy.

When the time came for her to make her plea before the King, she grew concerned that ceremonial law, coupled with the King's previous experience with an un-submissive wife might lead to her undoing. Mordecai, the only father figure she had known growing up, gave her the wise counsel that I believe echoes down through history to our listening ears:

"Do not think that because you are in the king's

house you alone of all the Jews will escape. For
if you remain silent at this time, relief and
deliverance for the Jews will arise from another
place, but you and your father's family will
perish. And who knows but that you have come
to your royal position for such a time as
this?"[159]

There's no questioning the fact that it is beyond easy for a
Christian believer in the United States today to become
discouraged. Simply go back to Chapter 1 and review the
events unfolding around us and how they eerily mirror those
described in the pages of Romans to recognize how desperate
of times we now live in. But let that also be an encouragement
to you. In the midst of Roman sin and excess, where was Paul?
Where was Silas? Where were Priscilla and Aquila? They were
serving God joyously as though they anticipated His return that
very day. They urgently carried the truth to every corner of the
known world because that was their calling, unaffected by the
actions or intrigues of men.

Fellow believers, God is not surprised by anything that is
happening in 21st Century America. Like the Master Chess
Player, He has been prepared for our cultural rebellion from
the beginning of time. And the way He prepared for it was to
position you and me right here, right now, for such a time as
this. Why? Because He trusts us to stand for truth and
righteousness without fear – being faithful servants no matter
what men may say or do. That isn't discouraging; it's inspiring.

Perhaps Jesus' closest companion while on the earth He
created, the Apostle Peter, reminds us:

"If you suffer as a Christian, do not be ashamed,
but praise God that you bear that name."[160]

I was walking through the grocery store not long ago,
trying desperately to find something called "evaporated milk."

222

STRANGERS

First of all, I was convinced Jenny had just made that up and was trying to get me to make a fool of myself by asking an employee where to find it. I was so sure of that fact that I spent at least 30 minutes searching for it myself before I eventually gave in and asked. Just FYI, it's real and in the baking goods section.

After concluding my search, I was heading towards the check-out when I ran into a young man who had attended one of our 414 Retreats. He spoke up right away and told me how very glad he was that he had attended. I was extremely encouraged to hear that, but also sorry that he had encountered some anti-Christian hostility so readily on campus. His response as we parted made me want to start conducting these retreats every weekend of the year in every state of the union. He looked back at me, shrugged and said, "They call us fools...let 'em." Then he smiled, and took off.

"Let 'em." Praise God.

The world lost an incredible mind and spirit in early 2016 when former U.S. Supreme Court Associate Justice Antonin Scalia died. Besides his irreplaceable contributions to American jurisprudence, Scalia was a firm believer in Jesus Christ. His timeless counsel to Christians has never been more appropriate than now:

> "God assumed from the beginning that the wise of the world would view Christians as fools...and He has not been disappointed. Devout Christians are destined to be regarded as fools in modern society. We are fools for Christ's sake...
>
> We must pray for courage to endure the scorn of the sophisticated world. If I have brought any message today, it is this: Have the courage to have your wisdom regarded as stupidity. Be

fools for Christ. And have the courage to suffer
the contempt of the sophisticated world."[161]

Amen. After all, we are strangers here. What else should
we expect?

CITATIONS

[1] Shapiro, Ben. "Rahm Emanuel Pledges to Ban Chick-fil-A from Chicago," *Breitbart News*, July 25, 2012. Online: http://www.breitbart.com/big-government/2012/07/25/rahm-emanuel-latest-to-fight-chick-fil-a/.

[2] Gockowski, Anthony. "UNK Refuses to Bring Chick-fil-A to Campus Over CEO's Marriage Views," Campus Reform, February 19, 2016. Online: http://www.campusreform.org/?ID=7310.

[3] Seleh, Pardes. "Chick-fil-A Banned from the University of Nebraska Because CEO Supports Traditional Marriage," *The Daily Wire*, February 18, 2016. Online: http://www.dailywire.com/news/3507/chick-fil-banned-university-nebraska-because-ceo-pardes-seleh.

[4] Hefner, Hugh. "10 Questions for Hugh Hefner," *Time Magazine*, 2016. Online: http://content.time.com/time/video/player/0,32068,7586064001_1872206,00.html.

[5] Lee, Lois. "2010 Founder's Hero of the Heart Award," *Children of the Night: Rescuing America's Children from Prostitution*, November 18, 2010. Online: https://www.childrenofthenight.org/pdf/Hugh_Hefner_Founders_Hero_of_the_Heart_Award.pdf.

[6] Editors of Biography.com. "Hugh Hefner Biography," *Biography.com*, February 25, 2016. Online: http://www.biography.com/people/hugh-hefner-9333521.

[7] Kittle, M.D. "Can Opposing Same-Sex Marriage Get Your Fired at Marquette University?" *The Daily Signal*, November 13, 2015. Online: http://dailysignal.com/2015/11/13/marriage-fired-marquette/.

[8] Craine, Patrick. "I Attended Ottawa's Gay Pride Parade. Here's What I Saw," *LifeSite*, September 6, 2013. Online: https://www.lifesitenews.com/news/i-attended-ottawa-pride.-heres-what-i-saw.

[9] Laughland, Oliver. "Is Pride Today About Gay Rights or Just Partying?" *The Guardian*, July 6, 2012. Online: http://www.theguardian.com/commentisfree/2012/jul/06/conversation-pride-gay-rights-party

[10] Selander, Eden. "Lawrence Krauss: God is Irrelevant," *ScienceNET*, May 10, 2015. Online: https://www.youtube.com/watch?v=Av-Zo_ptiOA.
[11] Heilpern, Will. "Trump Campaign: 11 Outrageous Quotes," *CNN Politics*, February 23, 2016. Online: http://www.cnn.com/2015/12/31/politics/gallery/donald-trump-campaign-quotes/.
[12] Ibid.
[13] Nothstine, Ray. "Trump: Why Do I Have to Repent or Ask Forgiveness If I Am Not Making Mistakes?" *Christian Post*, July 23, 2015. Online: http://www.christianpost.com/news/trump-why-do-i-have-to-repent-or-ask-for-forgiveness-if-i-am-not-making-mistakes-video-141856/.
[14] Nothstine, Ray. "Donald Trump: 'I'm Not Sure If I Ever Asked God's Forgiveness," *Christian Post*, July 20, 2015. Online: http://www.christianpost.com/news/donald-trump-im-not-sure-if-i-ever-asked-gods-forgiveness-141706/.
[15] Steinbeck, John. *America and Americans and Selected Nonfiction*, eds. Susan Shillinglaw and Jackson Benson (New York: Viking, 2002), 353.
[16] Ibid.
[17] *The Holy Bible*, Deuteronomy 8: 10-20.
[18] Newsweek Cover: The Decline and Fall of Christian America, April 5, 2009. Online: http://www.prnewswire.com/news-releases/newsweek-cover-the-decline-and-fall-of-christian-america-61731527.html.
[19] Whistleblower Cover: Why Are Christians Losing America? May 2, 2005. Online: http://www.wnd.com/2005/05/29803/.
[20] Terry, Ralph B. "A Discourse Analysis of First Corinthians: Aspects of Culture at Corinth," July 13, 2002. Online: http://bible.ovc.edu/terry/dissertation/2_4-aspects.htm.
[21] Lewis, C.S. *Mere Christianity* (1952; Harper Collins: 2001), pg 45-46.
[22] *The Holy Bible*, 1 Peter 1:1-2.
[23] *The Holy Bible*, John 14: 1-3.
[24] The Holy Bible, 1 Peter 1: 3-5.
[25] Pew Research Center, "America's Changing Religious Landscape," May 12, 2015. Online: http://www.pewforum.org/2015/05/12/americas-changing-religious-landscape/.

[26] Stetzer, Ed. "Barna: How Many Have a Biblical Worldview," *Christianity Today*, March 9, 2009. Online: http://www.christianitytoday.com/edstetzer/2009/march/barna-how-many-have-biblical-worldview.html.
[27] All comments visible online: https://www.instagram.com/p/7EYyQGOYv4/?taken-by=heck414.
[28] Lee, Morgan. "Wheaton Faculty Council Unanimously Asks College to Keep Larycia Hawkins," Christianity Today, January 21, 2016. Online: http://www.christianitytoday.com/gleanings/2016/january/wheaton-faculty-council-asks-college-keep-larycia-hawkins.html.
[29] PeterHeck.com. "Heck Spars with University President," June 23, 2014. Online: http://www.peterheck.com/peterheck/062314uts.
[30] The Holy Bible, 1 Peter 1: 6.
[31] Parti, Tarini. "FEC: $7B Spent on 2012 Campaign," *Politico*, January 31, 2013. Online: http://www.politico.com/story/2013/01/7-billion-spent-on-2012-campaign-fec-says-087051.
[32] Donohue, Joseph. "The Top 25 Most Expensive Local Races in New Jersey," *PolitickerNJ*, January 22, 2015. Online: http://politickernj.com/2015/01/elec-special-report-2014-12-6-million-newark-mayors-race-was-costliest-ever/.
[33] Lewis, C.S. Mere Christianity (New York: MacMillan Publishing Company, 1952).
[34] The Holy Bible, John 19:11.
[35] The Holy Bible, Acts 25:11.
[36] The Holy Bible, 1 Peter 1:6.
[37] The Holy Bible, Romans 1:18.
[38] Hodges, Mark. "Cincinnati Imposes Massive Fines on Counselors who Help Youth with Unwanted Gay Attractions," *LifeSiteNews*, December 8, 2015. Online: https://www.lifesitenews.com/news/homosexual-activists-council-members-use-deception-to-vote-against-reparati.
[39] Evans, Rachel H. Twitter post online: https://twitter.com/rachelheldevans/status/639505803272175616.
[40] Westen, John H. "Jailed Christian Clerk Kim Davis – A Hero, Not a Villain," *CNS News*, September 3, 2015. Online: http://www.cnsnews.com/commentary/john-henry-westen/jailed-christian-clerk-kim-davis-hero-not-villain.

[41] Snyder, Michael. "16 Cold Hard Facts That Prove That America Has Become a Nation Full of Perverts and Predators," *End of the American Dream*, February 2, 2010. Online: http://endoftheamericandream.com/archives/16-cold-hard-facts-that-prove-that-america-has-become-a-nation-full-of-perverts-and-predators.

[42] Snyder, Michael. "100 Facts About the Moral Collapse of America That Are Almost Too Crazy to Believe," *The Truth*, April 9, 2014. Online: http://thetruthwins.com/archives/100-facts-about-the-moral-collapse-of-america-that-are-almost-too-crazy-to-believe.

[43] Steiner, Bernard C. *The Life and Correspondence of James McHenry* (Cleveland: The Burrows Brothers, 1907), p. 475 (in a letter from Charles Carroll to James McHenry, November 4, 1800).

[44] The Holy Bible, Judges 2:10.

[45] Phillips, Craig & Dean. *I Want to be Just Like You*. Sparrow Records, 2013. CD.

[46] Atkins, Rodney, and Ted Hewitt. *Watching You*. Curb Records, 2010. CD.

[47] Chaput, Charles J. "Strangers in a Strange Land, 2014 Erasmus Lecture." *First Things*, January 2015. Online: http://www.firstthings.com/article/2015/01/strangers-in-a-strange-land.

[48] Ibid.

[49] The Holy Bible, John 17:14-19.

[50] The Holy Bible, Titus 3:7.

[51] The Holy Bible, Philippians 3:8-14.

[52] Block, Matthew. "The Spiritualist Origins of 'You Don't Have a Soul. You Are a Soul.'" *First Things*, January 13, 2014. Online: http://www.firstthings.com/blogs/firstthoughts/2014/01/the-spiritualist-origins-of-you-dont-have-a-soul-you-are-a-soul.

[53] Ibid.

[54] The Holy Bible, James 4:14.

[55] The Holy Bible, 1 Peter 1:6-9.

[56] Hewitt, Hugh. *In, But Not Of: A Guide to Christian Ambition and the Desire to Influence the World.* (Nashville: Thomas Nelson, 2012), pg. 203.

[57] Kirk, Marshall K. and Hunter Madsen. *After the Ball: How America Will Conquer its Fear and Hatred of Gays in the 90s.* (Penguin Books, 1989), pg. 147-157.

[58] Baume, Matt. What's the Real Definition of "Traditional Marriage?" *Huffington Post*, February 2, 2016. Online: http://www.huffingtonpost.com/matt-baume/whats-the-real-definition-of-traditional-marriage_b_7653172.html.

[59] Wax, Trevin. "Must Christianity Changes its Sexual Ethics? History May Hold the Key," Religion News, April 8, 2015. Online: http://www.religionnews.com/2015/04/08/must-christianity-change-sexual-ethics-history-may-hold-key-commentary/.

[60] Ibid.

[61] Ibid.

[62] Edwards, Jonathan. "Sinners in the Hands of an Angry God," Sermons and Discourses, 1739. (WJE Online Vol. 22). Online: http://edwards.yale.edu/archive?path=aHR0cDovL2Vkd2FyZIIMu eWFsZS5lZHUvY2dpLWJpbi9uZXdwaGlsby9nZXRvYmplY3QucGw/ Yy4yMToONy53amVv.

[63] Hewitt, Hugh. *In, But Not Of: A Guide to Christian Ambition and the Desire to Influence the World.* (Nashville: Thomas Nelson, 2012), pg. 194.

[64] The Holy Bible, Matthew 10:34.

[65] The Holy Bible, Matthew 5:46-47.

[66] Lewis, C.S. *The Weight of Glory.* (HarperOne, 2001), pg. 45-46.

[67] The Holy Bible, 1 Peter 2:11-12.

[68] The Holy Bible, 1 Corinthians 15:33.

[69] GotQuestions.org, "How Does Bad Company Corrupt Good Character?" Online: http://www.gotquestions.org/bad-company.html.

[70] The Holy Bible, 1 Corinthians 7:22.

[71] The Holy Bible, John 8:34.

[72] The Holy Bible, Proverbs 12:26.

[73] The Holy Bible, 2 Corinthians 6:14.

[74] The Holy Bible, Proverbs 13:20.

[75] The Holy Bible, Proverbs 14:7.

[76] The Holy Bible, Proverbs 22:24.

[77] The Holy Bible, Daniel 1: 1-6.

[78] The Holy Bible, Daniel 1: 8-14.

[79] The Holy Bible, Daniel 1: 7.

[80] The Holy Bible, Daniel 1: 15-20.

[81] The Holy Bible, Daniel 3: 1-2, 4-6.

[82] The Holy Bible, Daniel 3: 13-29.

[83] The Holy Bible, John 17: 13-18.

84 Mathis, David. "Let's Revise the Popular Phrase 'In, But Not Of.'" Desiring God, August 29, 2012. Online: http://www.desiringgod.org/articles/let-s-revise-the-popular-phrase-in-but-not-of.
85 The Holy Bible, Matthew 28: 19-20.
86 Wilberforce, Robert I. and Samuel Wilberforce (ed.), *The Life of William Wilberforce*, Cambridge: Cambridge University Press, 2011, pg. 10.
87 Hewitt, Hugh. *In, But Not Of: A Guide to Christian Ambition and the Desire to Influence the World.* Nashville: Thomas Nelson, 2012, pg. 20.
88 The Holy Bible, Matthew 10:16.
89 The Holy Bible, Matthew 10:22.
90 The Holy Bible, John 15:19.
91 Dawkins, Richard. *The God Delusion.* (London: Bantam Press, 2006), pg. 356.
92 Dawkins, pg. 357.
93 Barna Group. "Most American Christians Do Not Believe That Satan or the Holy Spirit Exist," *Research Releases in Faith & Christianity*, April 13, 2009. Online: https://www.barna.org/barna-update/faith-spirituality/260-most-american-christians-do-not-believe-that-satan-or-the-holy-spirit-exis#.VwP8bPQrIUs.
94 Webb, Lee. "Most Don't Believe in Hell," *CBN News*, March 28, 2007. Online: http://www.cbn.com/cbnnews/us/2007/march/most-dont-believe-in-hell/?mobile=false.
95 The Holy Bible, Matthew 25:41 and Revelation 20:10.
96 The Holy Bible, Matthew 13:41,50; Revelation 20:11-15, 21:8.
97 The Holy Bible, Matthew 13:50; Mark 9:48; Rev 14:10.
98 The Holy Bible, Revelation 14:11, 20:14-15.
99 Washer, Paul. "The True Gospel," *VCY America Rally for Youth*, Online: http://www.sermonaudio.com/viewtranscript.asp?sermonid=2908229120&loc=51704.
100 Eckman, Jim. "The Spirituality of Oprah Winfrey," Grace University Issues in Perspective, July 4, 2011. Online: https://graceuniversity.edu/iip/2011/06/04-1/.
101 The Holy Bible, John 14:6.
102 The Holy Bible, Acts 4:12.
103 The Holy Bible, Colossians 2:4.
104 The Holy Bible, Matthew 7:1.

[105] The Holy Bible, Matthew 7:1-5.
[106] The Holy Bible, 1 Corinthians 2:15.
[107] The Holy Bible, Hebrews 5:14.
[108] The Holy Bible, Matthew 7:16.
[109] Brown, Michael. "Jesus and Paul Call Us to Judge," Charisma News, May 19, 2015. Online: http://www.charismanews.com/opinion/in-the-line-of-fire/49698-jesus-and-paul-call-us-to-judge.
[110] The Holy Bible, Hebrews 12:14.
[111] Weber, Katherine. "Rob Bell Tells How 'Love Wins' Led to Mars Hill Departure," The Christian Post, December 3, 2012. Online: http://www.christianpost.com/news/rob-bell-tells-how-love-wins-led-to-mars-hill-departure-85995/.
[112] Gledhill, Ruth. "Tony Campolo Calls for Full Acceptance of Gay Christian Couples in the Church," Christianity Today, June 8, 2015. Online: http://www.christiantoday.com/article/tony.campolo.calls.for.full.acceptance.of.gay.christian.couples.in.the.church/55718.htm.
[113] Evans, Rachel H. "Want Millennials Back in the Pews? Stop Trying to Make Church 'Cool,'" Washington Post, April 30, 2015. Online: https://www.washingtonpost.com/opinions/jesus-doesnt-tweet/2015/04/30/fb07ef1a-ed01-11e4-8666-a1d756d0218e_story.html.
[114] McKinney, Amanda. "Proud Member of the Morality Police, At Your Service," Cultures at War, July 14, 2015. Online: https://culturesatwar.wordpress.com/2015/07/14/proud-member-of-the-morality-police-at-your-service/.
[115] Ibid.
[116] Scholtes, Peter. "They'll Know We Are Christians By Our Love," Jars of Clay, The Lorenz Corporation. Online: http://www.metrolyrics.com/theyll-know-we-are-christians-by-our-love-lyrics-jars-of-clay.html.
[117] The Holy Bible, John 13:35.
[118] The Holy Bible, Luke 12:51.
[119] The Holy Bible, Luke 11:11.
[120] The Holy Bible, Matthew 28:20.
[121] The Holy Bible, Proverbs 16:25.
[122] The Holy Bible, Luke 5:22-24.
[123] The Holy Bible, Matthew 22:39.

[124] Castellitto, A.J. "Peace and Goodwill in an Age of Progressive Propaganda," *BarbWire*, December 25, 2015. Online: http://barbwire.com/2015/12/25/peace-and-goodwill/.
[125] The Holy Bible, 2 Timothy 2:14.
[126] The Holy Bible, 2 Timonthy 2:15
[127] The Holy Bible, Acts 17:2-4.
[128] Hitchens, Christopher. *Letters to a Young Contrarian.* (Cambridge: Basic Books, 2001).
[129] The Holy Bible, 2 Corinthians 10:5.
[130] The Holy Bible, Exodus 4:10.
[131] The Holy Bible, Exodus 4:11-12.
[132] The Holy Bible, 2 Timothy 2:15.
[133] Hewitt, Hugh. *In, But Not Of* (Nashville: Thomas Nelson, 2003), 172-173.
[134] The Holy Bible, Galatians 6:14.
[135] The Holy Bible, Ecclesiastes 1:14.
[136] Douglass, Frederick. "The Hypocrisy of American Slavery," July 4, 1852. Great Speeches Collection. Online: http://www.historyplace.com/speeches/douglass.htm.
[137] The Holy Bible, Proverbs 26:4-6.
[138] Ramsey, Thor. "How is Sacrasm Helpful," January 28, 2016. Online: https://thorramseydotcom.wordpress.com/2016/01/28/how-is-sarcasm-helpful/.
[139] Ibid.
[140] Koukl, Gregory. *Tactics.* (Grand Rapids: Zondervan, 2009), pg. 31.
[141] The Holy Bible, 2 Corinthians 10:5.
[142] The Holy Bible, John 10:27.
[143] The Holy Bible, 1 Peter 3:15.
[144] Koukl, Gregory. *Tactics.* (Grand Rapids: Zondervan, 2009), pg. 27.
[145] Emmerich, Roland, dir. *The Patriot.* Written Robert Rodat. Columbia Pictures, 2000. Film.
[146] Koukl, Gregory. *Tactics.* (Grand Rapids: Zondervan, 2009), pg. 39.
[147] Koukl, Gregory. *Tactics.* (Grand Rapids: Zondervan, 2009), pg. 46.
[148] Koukl, pg. 46-47.
[149] Koukl, pg. 47.
[150] The Holy Bible, Ecclesiastes 1:9.

[151] The Holy Bible, Colossians 2:4.
[152] This entire Facebook conversation is visible, unedited with third-party comments included online at: www.peterheck.com/peterheck/strangersprof.
[153] Lewontin, Richard. "Billions and Billions of Demons," *New York Review of Books*, January 4, 1997.
[154] Ibid.
[155] Ibid.
[156] Koukl, Gregory. *Tactics*. (Grand Rapids: Zondervan, 2009), pg. 51.
[157] Koukl, pg. 60-61.
[158] Keyes, Alan. *Our Character, Our Future*. (Grand Rapids: Zondervan, 1996).
[159] The Holy Bible, Esther 4:13-14.
[160] The Holy Bible, 1 Peter 4:16.
[161] Draper, Electa. "Justice Scalia Tells Catholics to Brave the Scorn of Worldly People," *The Denver Post*, March 3, 2012. Online: http://www.denverpost.com/ci_20095806.

ACKNOWLEDGEMENTS

Special acknowledgements to Gregory Koukl (*Tactics*) and Hugh Hewitt (*In, But Not Of*) for their contributions to many of the themes discussed in this book. If you enjoyed *Strangers*, you will love their work. If you didn't enjoy *Strangers*, give them a chance to redeem your faith in mankind.

Thanks to Parker Creative Services for logo and cover design. Spectacular as always.

Made in the USA
Lexington, KY
07 September 2017